P9-DGH-039

I'M NOT ANTI-BUSINESS, I'M ANTI-IDIOT

A DILBERT® BOOK

BY SCOTT ADAMS

Andrews McMeel Publishing
Kansas City

DILBERT® is a registered trademark of United Feature Syndicate, Inc.

DOGBERT and DILBERT appear in the comic strip DILBERT®, distributed by United Feature Syndicate, Inc.

http://www.unitedmedia.com/comics/dilbert

I'm Not Anti-Business, I'm Anti-Idiot copyright © 1998 United Feature Syndicate, Inc. All rights reserved. Printed in the United States of America. No part of this book may be used or reproduced in any manner whatsoever without written permission except in the case of reprints in the context of reviews. For information, write Andrews McMeel Publishing, an Andrews McMeel Universal company, 4520 Main Street, Kansas City, Missouri 64111.

www.andrewsmcmeel.com

98 99 00 01 02 BAH 10 9 8 7 6 5 4 3 2 1

ISBN: 0-8362-5182-2

Library of Congress Catalog Card Number: 97-80772

ATTENTION: SCHOOLS AND BUSINESSES

Andrews McMeel books are available at quantity discounts with bulk purchase for educational, business, or sales promotional use. For information, please write to: Special Sales Department, Andrews McMeel Publishing, 4520 Main Street, Kansas City, Missouri 64111.

Blah, blah, blah, Pam. Blah, blah, blah.

Other DILBERT Books from Andrews McMeel Publishing

Seven Years of Highly Defective People
ISBN: 0-8362-3668-8

Casual Day Has Gone Too Far
ISBN: 0-8362-2899-5

Fugitive from the Cubicle Police
ISBN: 0-8362-2119-2

Still Pumped from Using the Mouse
ISBN: 0-8362-1026-3

It's Obvious You Won't Survive By Your Wits Alone
ISBN: 0-8362-0415-8

Bring Me the Head of Willy the Mailboy!
ISBN: 0-8362-1779-9

Shave the Whales
ISBN: 0-8362-1740-3

Dogbert's Clues for the Clueless
ISBN: 0-8362-1737-3

Build a Better Life by Stealing Office Supplies
ISBN: 0-8362-1757-8

Always Postpone Meetings with Time-Wasting Morons
ISBN: 0-8362-1758-6

For ordering information, call 1-800-642-6480.

Introduction

I'm a misunderstood cartoonist.

The people who misunderstand me the most are the ones who write to tell me they enthusiastically agree with my opinions. Those people scare me. Sometimes they develop irrational attractions to me, based on the fact that our opinions are so similar. They often inquire about the possibilities of mating with me, or—if they are male—drugging me and keeping me in a basement in a big glass container. It's all very flattering.

Other people write to tell me they plan to hunt me down and beat me senseless with ceramic statues because my opinions are at odds with their own well-constructed views of the universe. The people who worship unicorns come to mind. They're a vindictive group.

Still other people call me a hypocrite because their incomplete information about my actions is inconsistent with their misinterpretation of my opinions. I deal with this the only way I know how to—by signing their names to anti-unicorn literature.

The problem with other people's opinions about my opinions is that no one actually knows my opinions. All anyone knows about me is the dialogue I put in the mouths of rotund engineers, talking rats, megalomaniac dogs, and pointy-haired bosses. I might be dumb, but I'm not dumb enough to express my true opinion about anything important. The one thing I've learned about freedom of expression is that you really ought to keep that sort of thing to yourself.

That said, I do feel an irrational need to make one futile attempt to clear up the biggest misconception about my opinions: I'm not anti-*management*. I'm anti-*idiot*. The two groups intersect so often that I use the terms interchangeably, even though I know I shouldn't. Let me set the record straight: If you think you're a smart manager, you have my word that I'm only making fun of other people.*

Sincerely,

S. Adams

Scott Adams

*Unless you worship unicorns.

S. Adams 11/20 © 1995 United Feature Syndicate, Inc.(NYC)

S. Adams 11/21 © 1995 United Feature Syndicate, Inc.(NYC)

S. Adams 11/22 © 1995 United Feature Syndicate, Inc.(NYC)

THE COMPANY HAS DECIDED TO OUTSOURCE ALL OF THE FUNCTIONS THAT WE'RE NOT ANY GOOD AT.

Yippee!
Yay!
S.Adams

WHEN'S YOUR LAST DAY?
UH-OH...THEY'RE NOT GOOD AT KNOWING WHAT THEY'RE NOT GOOD AT...
11/23 © 1995 United Feature Syndicate, Inc.(NYC)

I DON'T UNDERSTAND WHY SOME PEOPLE WASH THEIR BATH TOWELS.

WHEN I GET OUT OF THE SHOWER I'M THE CLEANEST OBJECT IN MY HOUSE. IN THEORY, THOSE TOWELS SHOULD BE GETTING CLEANER EVERY TIME THEY TOUCH ME.
S.Adams

MAYBE I COULD HUG YOU EVERY DAY SO I DON'T NEED TO TAKE SHOWERS.
ARE TOWELS SUPPOSED TO BEND?
11/24 © 1995 United Feature Syndicate, Inc.(NYC)

I'VE GOTTA RUN TO THE POST OFFICE.

YOU GO TO THE POST OFFICE EVERY DAY. ARE YOU AWARE THAT YOU CAN BUY MORE THAN ONE STAMP AT A TIME?
S.Adams

APPARENTLY YOU DON'T UNDERSTAND THE CONCEPT OF "FLOAT."
11/25 © 1995 United Feature Syndicate, Inc.(NYC)

© 1995 United Feature Syndicate, Inc. (NYC)

MY PASSWORD FOR THE NETWORK ISN'T WORKING
FILL OUT A A HELP REQUEST ONLINE.
S. Adams

I CAN'T GET ONLINE BECAUSE MY PASSWORD DOESN'T WORK...
SEND ME AN E-MAIL MESSAGE ABOUT IT.

I CAN'T SEND E-MAIL BECAUSE I CAN'T GET ON THE STINKIN' NETWORK!!!
GEEZ, YOU'RE WORTHLESS...
11/27 © 1995 United Feature Syndicate, Inc.(NYC)

DOES HUMAN RESOURCES OFFER ANY TREATMENT PROGRAMS FOR PEOPLE WITH DYSFUNCTIONAL INTERNET CONNECTIONS?
S. Adams

I RECOMMEND THE "YARN THERAPY." YOU'LL BE WRAPPED IN A HUGE BALL OF YARN AND USED AS FURNITURE IN MY OFFICE.

IS THIS LIKE THE FAMOUS "ROPES" COURSE WHERE I LEARN TO SOLVE PROBLEMS AS PART OF A TEAM?
EXACTLY, EXCEPT HERE YOU LEARN TO BE MY COUCH.
11/28 © 1995 United Feature Syndicate, Inc.(NYC)

ALICE, DID YOU HEAR THAT DILBERT'S NETWORK CONNECTION ISN'T WORKING?
UH-OH
S. Adams

HE IS WHAT WE CALL A TECHNOLOGY "HAVE NOT." HIS COMPETITIVENESS IN THE GLOBAL ECONOMY WILL LAST AS LONG AS THIS FRENCH FRY.
SO SAD.

AFTER LUNCH, I'M GOING TO USE SOMETHING CALLED "ELECTRONIC MAIL." YOU CAN WATCH IF YOU PROMISE NOT TO TOUCH ANY-THING.
SNORK!
GULP
11/29 © 1995 United Feature Syndicate, Inc.(NYC)

WE'VE BEEN DATING FOR A YEAR NOW, LIZ. THERE'S SOMETHING I'D LIKE TO DO TONIGHT...

THERE ARE SOME NEEDS THAT I CAN'T FULFILL AT WORK.
I UNDER-STAND.
S. Adams

YES! YES!
HOW LONG HAS YOUR INTERNET CONNECTION AT WORK BEEN BROKEN?
11/30 © 1995 United Feature Syndicate, Inc.(NYC)

WE JUST SHIPPED OUR NEWEST PRODUCT. YOU FOLKS IN TECH SUPPORT WILL NEED TO BE TRAINED SO YOU CAN AVOID ANY EMBARRASSMENTS.

WE HAD A MONK WRITE THE TRAINING MATERIAL ON A GRAIN OF RICE. WE COULD ONLY AFFORD ONE, SO YOU'LL HAVE TO SHARE IT.
S. Adams

TO BE HONEST, I'M NOT SURE WE HAD A REAL MONK. HE WROTE EVERY-THING IN PIG LATIN.
12/1 © 1995 United Feature Syndicate, Inc.(NYC)

DOES YOUR BOSS GIVE YOU ORDERS AND LATER DENY IT? DO YOU GET IN TROUBLE FOR DOING WHAT YOU'RE TOLD?
YES

THE "DOGBERT DETECTIVE AGENCY" WILL VIDEOTAPE IT ALL AND EMBARRASS YOUR BOSS WITH PROOF!
S. Adams

WHAT??! WHY DID YOU DO THIS??!
THIS IS THE HAPPIEST MOMENT OF MY CAREER.
LIGHTS!
12/2 © 1995 United Feature Syndicate, Inc.(NYC)

WORKING LATE AGAIN, HUH, ALICE?
SEVENTY HOURS THIS WEEK...
S. ADAMS
ME TOO. THANK GOODNESS FOR OVERTIME PAY!
OVERTIME PAY?
ALLOW ME TO EXPLAIN.
UNLIKE YOU SO-CALLED "EXEMPT" EMPLOYEES, MY INCOME INCREASES IF I WORK ADDITIONAL HOURS.
$
Hours
© 1995 United Feature Syndicate, Inc. (NYC)
I'M PULLING IN SEVENTY-FIVE THOUSAND A YEAR. AND HALF THE TIME I JUST HIDE IN THE BASEMENT READING "FISHING" MAGAZINE.
THE ONLY DOWN SIDE IS THAT I DON'T GET TO ENJOY THE INTELLECTUAL STIMULATION OF MY CO-WORKERS THE WAY YOU DO.
12/3
I DON'T KNOW WHAT I LIKE BETTER — DEEP SEA FISHING OR CUBICLE FISHING.
FISH

ON ONE HAND, MY COMPANY DOES USE INFERIOR TECHNOLOGY IN OUR PRODUCTS...
S.Adams

BUT ON THE OTHER HAND, I'M THE MOST ATTRACTIVE FEMALE WHO HAS PAID ATTENTION TO YOU THIS YEAR.

12/4 © 1995 United Feature Syndicate, Inc.(NYC)
WHAT KIND OF ENGINEERS DO YOU THINK WE ARE??!
DO YOU HAVE PICTURES OF YOUR FIELD SUPPORT PEOPLE?

I CAN'T BELIEVE YOU'RE RECOMMENDING THIS LOUSY VENDOR JUST BECAUSE THE SALES REP IS GORGEOUS.
S.Adams

HERE'S A PICTURE OF THOR, THEIR FIELD ENGINEER.

12/5 © 1995 United Feature Syndicate, Inc.(NYC)
DOES HE REALLY WORK WITHOUT A SHIRT?
ONLY IF YOU BUY THE "INDIAN CHIEF" MAINTENANCE PACKAGE.

YOUR EMPLOYEES HAVE RECOMMENDED A VENDOR WHO HAS AN ATTRACTIVE SALESPERSON.

BUT THE "DOGBERT TECHNOLOGY COMPANY" CAN PROVIDE YOU WITH A HARDWARE SOLUTION FOR HALF THE COST!
I'LL SAVE MONEY!
S.Adams

12/6 © 1995 United Feature Syndicate, Inc.(NYC)
WHAT IF I NEED TO UPGRADE LATER? IS IT EXPENSIVE?
I MUST HAVE LEFT THAT PRICE SHEET IN MY OTHER FUR.

SO, YOU IGNORED MY RECOMMENDATION AND BOUGHT A LOW-COST SYSTEM THAT'S TOTALLY INADEQUATE...
S. Adams

YOU COMPENSATED FOR THIS BLUNDER BY MAKING IT PART OF MY OBJECTIVES TO MAKE THE SYSTEM WORK...

YOU'LL GET A BONUS FOR SAVING MONEY. I'LL GET FIRED, THUS SAVING MORE MONEY AND EARNING YOU ANOTHER BONUS.
I'M ON A ROLL.
12/7 © 1995 United Feature Syndicate, Inc.(NYC)

IT'S FUNNY – BEFORE YOUR COMPANY BOUGHT THAT CRITICAL SYSTEM FROM ME, YOU HAD ALL THE POWER...
S. Adams

BUT NOW, ONLY I CAN PROVIDE ESSENTIAL UPGRADES!! I CALL THE SHOTS, YOU SIMPLE FOOL!!

SEND IN THE NEXT EMPLOYEE.
AT LEAST WE DON'T HAVE ANY MULTI-VENDOR COMPATIBILITY ISSUES.
12/8 © 1995 United Feature Syndicate, Inc.(NYC)

IT'S INEXPLICABLE, BUT THE LOW-COST SYSTEM I SOLD YOU SEEMS TO BE WOEFULLY UNDER-POWERED.
S. Adams

YOU COULD REPLACE IT WITH ANOTHER VENDOR'S SYSTEM, THUS SHOWING EVERYBODY YOU MADE A MISTAKE. OR YOU CAN PAY MY OUTRAGEOUS UPGRADE FEES.

HOW BIG A FOOL DO YOU THINK I AM?
I WON'T KNOW UNTIL I SEE IF YOU GO FOR THE LEASE OPTION.
12/9 © 1995 United Feature Syndicate, Inc.(NYC)

HELLO, IS THIS THE "HELP DESK"?
NO, THAT GROUP GOT REENGINEERED OUT OF EXISTENCE.
S. Adams
I'M THE NEW "NO HELP WHATSOEVER DESK." MY JOB IS TO MAKE SURE YOU NEVER CALL AGAIN.
CAN YOU TELL ME HOW TO MAKE A PIE CHART?
CRUSH YOUR COMPUTER INTO SMALL CHUNKS, ADD FLOUR AND BAKE ONE HOUR.
© 1995 United Feature Syndicate, Inc. (NYC)
12/10
WHILE YOU'RE WAITING, READ THE FREE NOVEL WE SENT YOU. IT'S A SPANISH STORY ABOUT A GUY NAMED "MANUAL."
REPEAT THE PROCESS UNTIL YOU GET THE DESIRED RESULT.
THIS LOST A LOT IN THE TRANSLATION.
MANUAL

S. Adams 12/11 © 1995 United Feature Syndicate, Inc.(NYC)

S. Adams 12/12 © 1995 United Feature Syndicate, Inc.(NYC)

S. Adams 12/13 © 1995 United Feature Syndicate, Inc.(NYC)

WAIT-A-MINUTE... I'M STARTING TO REALIZE SOMETHING.
MY JOB TITLE IS SENIOR ASSOCIATE, YET I SPEND MY TIME DOING CLERICAL WORK... AND UNLESS I'M MISTAKEN, I'M THE LOWEST PAID EMPLOYEE.
S. Adams
IS THIS A BAD TIME?
AAAGH!! I'M A SECRETARY!
12/14 © 1995 United Feature Syndicate, Inc.(NYC)

I READ SOMEWHERE THAT CERTAIN RELIGIONS REQUIRE THEIR INITIATES TO PERFORM POINTLESS NEVER-ENDING TASKS TO RID THEM OF THEIR EGOS.
S. Adams
12/15 © 1995 United Feature Syndicate, Inc.(NYC)
WHAT NOW?

WHEN I CONQUER THE WORLD I'LL HAVE A SECRET HANDSHAKE TO IDENTIFY THE PEOPLE WHO WILL BE PART OF MY NEW RULING CLASS.
CROSS YOUR EYES AND STICK OUT YOUR TONGUE. GOOD, NOW VIGOROUSLY SLAP YOUR FACE.
S. Adams
12/16 © 1995 United Feature Syndicate, Inc.(NYC)
THE PEOPLE WHO AREN'T DOING THAT WILL BE IDENTIFIED AS MY NEW RULING CLASS.
SLAP!

ALICE, OUR RECORDS SHOW THAT YOU HAVEN'T TAKEN A VACATION ALL YEAR.
COMPANY POLICY REQUIRES YOU TO USE YOUR VACATION DAYS.
S. Adams
HOW?? YOU TOLD ME TO WORK SEVEN DAYS A WEEK TO PREPARE THE PROJECT FOR YOUR BOSS'S YEAR-END REVIEW.
© 1995 United Feature Syndicate, Inc.(NYC)
DO YOU WANT ME TO MEET THE ARTIFICIAL PROJECT TARGET OR THE ARTIFICIAL VACATION TARGET?
HELLO!!! THESE ARE MUTUALLY EXCLUSIVE GOALS!!! HELLO!!!
OOH... SORRY. I USUALLY JUST THINK THAT LAST PART IN SILENT FRUSTRATION.
12/17/95
MOVING RIGHT ALONG... KUDOS TO WALLY FOR USING ALL OF HIS VACATION DAYS AHEAD OF SCHEDULE.
GET OVER IT, ALICE. WE CAN'T ALL BE SUPERSTARS.

12/18 © 1995 United Feature Syndicate, Inc.(NYC)

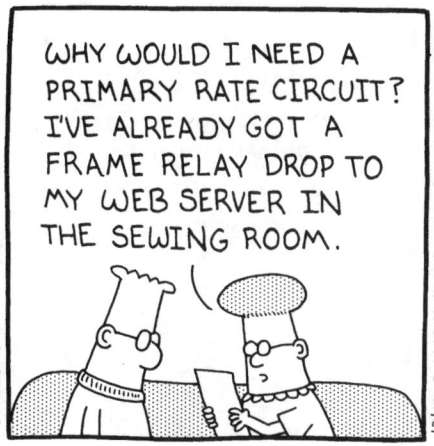

12/19 © 1995 United Feature Syndicate, Inc.(NYC)

12/20 © 1995 United Feature Syndicate, Inc.(NYC)

IT ISN'T ETHICAL TO HACK INTO THE PAYROLL COMPUTER AND GIVE ME A RAISE, DOGBERT.

NOT ETHICAL?? IS IT ETHICAL FOR THEM TO MAKE YOU WORK SEVENTY HOURS A WEEK AND ONLY PAY YOU FOR FORTY??!!
S.Adams

HOW ABOUT A FIVE PERCENT RAISE?
WELL, THERE IS THE ISSUE OF THE QUALITY OF YOUR WORK...
12/21 © 1995 United Feature Syndicate, Inc.(NYC)

MOST BUSINESS PLANS FAIL. OBVIOUSLY, SUCCESS IS NOT A REALISTIC GOAL.

BUT THE PEOPLE WHO MANAGE THE MOST SPECTACULAR FAILURES GET PROMOTED FIRST BECAUSE OF THEIR EXPERIENCE.
S.Adams

THAT IS THE MOST CYNICAL THING I'VE EVER HEARD IN MY LIFE!
THANKS. I'M BLUSHING.
12/22 © 1995 United Feature Syndicate, Inc.(NYC)

ON THE ADVICE OF MY DOG, I'M ASKING FOR AN ADDITIONAL TEN MILLION DOLLARS FOR MY PROJECT.

THAT WILL MAKE A MORE SPECTACULAR FAILURE, THUS GUARANTEEING A PROMOTION FOR ME.
AS YOUR BOSS, I'D GET RECOGNITION TOO...OKAY.
S.Adams

WOW! DO YOU HAVE ANY ADVICE FOR ME?!
BREATH MINTS.
12/23 © 1995 United Feature Syndicate, Inc.(NYC)

Happy Airlines
VACATION, HERE WE COME!
CLICK CLICK CLICK CLICK CLICK CLICK CLICK CLICK CLICK CLICK
S. Adams
WHY DO THEY HAVE TO ENTER SO MUCH STUFF IN THE COMPUTER?
CLICK CLICK CLICK CLICK CLICK CLICK CLICK
THEY ALREADY HAVE OUR RESERVATION AND SEAT ASSIGNMENT IN THERE. WHAT ELSE DO THEY NEED?
CLICK CLICK CLICK CLICK CLICK CLICK
I'M DEVELOPING A SUDDEN FEAR OF FLYING.
CLICK CLICK CLICK CLICK CLICK CLICK CLICK CLICK CLICK CLICK CLICK CLICK
STEP ASIDE.
12/24/95
WHAT'S GOING ON UP HERE ??!!
GATE 13. HAVE A NICE FLIGHT.
OKAY.
© 1995 United Feature Syndicate, Inc.(NYC)
"THEY NEVER SAW THEIR BELOVED LUGGAGE AGAIN. THE MISFITS ALWAYS REGRETTED OFFENDING TANTRA, THE GODDESS OF FLIGHT. THE END."
CLICK CLICK CLICK CLICK

I GOT MYSELF ONE OF THOSE "900" PHONE NUMBERS. I MAKE MONEY EVERY TIME SOMEBODY CALLS FOR MY VALUABLE ADVICE.
S.Adams

RING RING RING RING RING RING

DO YOU EVER ANSWER IT?
VOICE MAIL... GET WITH THE NINETIES.
12/4/95 © 1995 United Feature Syndicate, Inc.

THIS IS A LIVING DOCUMENT.
S.Adams

AAAAH!!

NEXT TIME, JUST SAY YOU PLAN TO UPDATE IT.
MINE'S DEAD.
© 1995 United Feature Syndicate, Inc.
12/26/95

OKAY! THIS IS ONE TIDY LITTLE CUBICLE NOW!
DILBERT
TRASH

THE CLEANLINESS OF ONE'S WORK SPACE IS A SIGN OF HOW MUCH ONE ENJOYS ONE'S JOB.
DILBERT
S.Adams

GIVE ME THE CLEANER; IT'S MY TURN TO FANTASIZE THAT I'M A MAID.
FIVE MORE MINUTES... PLEASE.
12/27/95 © 1995 United Feature Syndicate, Inc.(NYC)

I DECLARE MYSELF "KING DOGBERT," THE FIRST RULER OF THE INTERNET!!
S.Adams

BOW BEFORE ME OR BE EXPELLED FROM THE KINGDOM FOREVER!!!

ARE YOU AWARE THAT THE INTERNET IS COMPRISED OF MILLIONS OF INDIVIDUALS AND ORGANIZATIONS THAT OPERATE INDEPENDENTLY?
UNTIL NOW!
12/29/95 © 1995 United Feature Syndicate, Inc.(NYC)

YOUR NEW SOFTWARE IS SUCCESSFULLY INSTALLED. DO YOU WANT TO SEND YOUR REGISTRATION INFO BY MODEM?
YES
S.Adams

THE SOFTWARE HAS FOUND YOUR CREDIT CARD NUMBER AND IS PLACING ORDERS FOR NEW PRODUCTS IT THINKS YOU NEED... PLEASE WAIT.
UH...

MAKING ROOM ON YOUR HARD DRIVE...
I CAN'T TELL IF IT'S A VIRUS OR JUST EXCELLENT MARKETING.
EITHER WAY...
12/27/95 © 1995 United Feature Syndicate, Inc.

CORRECTION
A RECENT DILBERT STRIP USED THE WORDS "ANT FARM" TO DESCRIBE A HABITAT FOR ANTS.
S.Adams

LAWYERS HAVE INFORMED ME THAT "ANT FARM" IS A TRADEMARK OF "UNCLE MILTON INDUSTRIES, INC." THEY DEMAND A PUBLIC CLARIFICATION.
12/30 © 1995 United Feature Syndicate, Inc.(NYC)

WHAT SHOULD WE CALL A HABITAT FOR WORTHLESS AND DISGUSTING LITTLE CREATURES?
LAW SCHOOL.

I'VE GOT AN IDEA!
WE'RE DOOMED.
WHY CAN'T WE RUN OUR INVENTORY DATABASE OVER OUR E-MAIL SYSTEM?
S. Adams
FACT: THAT IS THE STUPIDEST IDEA IN THE UNIVERSE.
FACT: HIS COMPREHENSION IS SO LIMITED THAT DEBATE IS FUTILE.
FACT: WE COULD SPEND HOURS UNSUCCESSFULLY EXPLAINING WHY IT'S A STUPID IDEA.
12/31/95 © 1995 United Feature Syndicate, Inc. (NYC)
FACT: HE WOULD NEVER KNOW IF WE USED HIS IDEA OR NOT.
NO PROBLEM.
WE'LL GET RIGHT ON IT.
MY WORK IS DONE.
STUPIDITY IS LIKE NUCLEAR POWER; IT CAN BE USED FOR GOOD OR EVIL.
AND YOU DON'T WANT TO GET ANY ON YOU.

A WHILE BACK I ASKED FOR OPINIONS ABOUT THIS NEW CHARACTER, "TINA THE BRITTLE TECH WRITER."
RRRR
S. Adams
RESULTS
MOST PEOPLE, INCLUDING NEARLY ALL SELF-DESCRIBED FEMINISTS, SAID KEEP HER. BUT THERE WERE MANY REQUESTS TO ADD "NON-STEREOTYPICAL" FEMALE CHARACTERS FOR BALANCE.
1/1/96 © 1995 United Feature Syndicate, Inc. (NYC)
IN THE INTEREST OF BALANCE I GIVE YOU "ANTINA."
IS ANYBODY UP FOR SOME MATH?

HI, I'M ANTINA THE NON-STEREOTYPICAL WOMAN.
S. Adams
THAT COMPUTER MONITOR YOU'RE USING IS SUPPOSED TO BE 17 INCHES. BUT IT'S MORE LIKE 16.5 INCHES.
1/2/96 © 1995 United Feature Syndicate, Inc. (NYC)
I TOOK THE COFFEE MACHINE APART JUST FOR FUN— WANT TO SEE?

I'VE DECIDED TO MASK MY BOYISH LOOKS BY GROWING A BEARD.
S. Adams
I DIDN'T THINK TED WAS SMART ENOUGH TO KNOW HOW TO GROW A BEARD.
HEE HEE
1/3/96 © 1995 United Feature Syndicate, Inc. (NYC)
TWO WEEKS LATER
HOW DO YOU LIKE MY BEARD?
MY SEARCH FOR A NEW MANAGER IS OVER.

1/4/96 © 1995 United Feature Syndicate, Inc. (NYC)

1/5/96 © 1995 United Feature Syndicate, Inc. (NYC)

1/6/96 © 1995 United Feature Syndicate, Inc. (NYC)

WHY DO I HAVE A FEELING OF IMPENDING DOOM?
GOOD NEWS!
UH-OH.
YOU WON'T HAVE TO SPEND ANOTHER LONELY DAY IN THIS TINY CUBICLE.
I'M GETTING AN OFFICE?
BETTER! YOU'RE GETTING A ROOMMATE!
WHY??? WE'VE GOT PLENTY OF EMPTY CUBICLES! OUR COMPANY OWNS THE WHOLE BUILDING!
© 1995 United Feature Syndicate, Inc.(NY'C)
1/7/96
THE FINANCE DEPARTMENT CHARGES MY BUDGET FOR THE SQUARE FOOTAGE WE USE.
IT'S A FALSE SAVINGS! YOU'RE HURTING THE COMPANY!
ALL I HEAR IS A FAINT BUZZING.
S. Adams
OH, WELL. HOW BAD COULD IT BE?
I HOPE YOU LIKE BAKED BEANS AND SQUARE-DANCING AS MUCH AS I DO!
BEANS

S. Adams

1/9/96 © 1996 United Feature Syndicate, Inc.(NYC)

S. Adams

1/9/96 © 1996 United Feature Syndicate, Inc.(NYC)

S. Adams

1/10/96 © 1996 United Feature Syndicate, Inc.(NYC)

S. Adams
1/11/96 © 1996 United Feature Syndicate, Inc.(NYC)

S. Adams
1/12/96 © 1996 United Feature Syndicate, Inc.(NYC)

S. Adams
1/13/96 © 1996 United Feature Syndicate, Inc.(NYC)

© 1995 United Feature Syndicate, Inc. (NYC)

I CALL MY NEW OPERATING SYSTEM THE "DOGBERT 2000."

SOON I WILL DOMINATE THE ENTIRE PC INDUSTRY! HEH-HEH...
IT LOOKS LIKE "WINDOWS 95."
S. Adams

I USE SOME OF THE SAME GRAPHIC METAPHORS, BUT I PRONOUNCE THEM DIFFERENTLY.
HOW DO YOU PRONOUNCE THE "MICROSOFT" LOGO?
1/15/96 © 1996 United Feature Syndicate, Inc.(NYC)

AFTER I BECOME A BILLIONAIRE FROM MY SOFTWARE COMPANY I'LL DO A LITTLE DANCE.

I'M SO RICH
IT'S ME YOU HAIL
IF I'M OBNOXIOUS
KISS MY TAIL
S. Adams

DO YOU PLAN TO DO ANY CHARITY WORK?
LET ME PUT IT THIS WAY— YOU JUST SAW MY CONTRIBUTION TO THE FINE ARTS.
1/16/96 © 1996 United Feature Syndicate, Inc.(NYC)

IF YOU PLAN TO REMAIN IN THE COMPUTER BUSINESS YOU'D BETTER BUNDLE THE "DOGBERT 2000" OPERATING SYSTEM WITH EVERY UNIT YOU SELL.

OTHERWISE, AFTER I DOMINATE THE MARKET YOU'LL BE LAST ON MY LIST TO RECEIVE NEW PRODUCTS!
S. Adams

YOU REMIND ME OF SOMEBODY...
IT'S THE GLASSES, ISN'T IT?
1/17/96 © 1996 United Feature Syndicate, Inc.(NYC)

DOGBERT MEETS WITH SOFTWARE DEVELOPERS
NOTE THE HUGE MARKET FOR SOFTWARE THAT RUNS ON THE "DOGBERT 2000" OPERATING SYSTEM.
S. Adams
BUT WHO CARES? THE IMPORTANT THING IS THAT I BROUGHT A BAG OF TOYS.
1/18/96 © 1996 United Feature Syndicate, Inc.(NYC)
SOME SAY THE COMPUTER INDUSTRY IS BUILT ON SILICON. I THINK FOAM AND PLASTIC ARE EQUALLY IMPORTANT.

THANKS TO MY SOFTWARE EMPIRE, MY NET WEALTH IS TWENTY BILLION DOLLARS.
S. Adams
CONTRARY TO POPULAR OPINION, IT DOES SEEM TO MAKE ME HAPPY.
1/19/96 © 1996 United Feature Syndicate, Inc.(NYC)
MONEY CAN'T BUY A SUNSET, DOGBERT.
NO, BUT I WAS ABLE TO LICENSE THE DIGITAL RIGHTS.

I HEARD YOU WERE DOING SOME BABY-SITTING, BOB.
YEAH! I DID THE MORTON TRIPLETS LAST NIGHT.
S. Adams
IT'S NOT EASY TO JUGGLE THREE SCREAMING TODDLERS.
1/20/96 © 1996 United Feature Syndicate, Inc.(NYC)
WHEN YOU SAY "JUGGLE"...
IT'S THE MORTONS WITH A QUESTION ABOUT THEIR CEILING FAN.

HEE HEE! THIS IS MY MOST DIABOLICAL WORK YET AS DIRECTOR OF HUMAN RESOURCES.
THANKS TO E-MAIL I CAN PLAY WITH HUNDREDS OF EMPLOYEES AT ONCE!
S. ADAMS
UH-OH... A MESSAGE FROM THE EVIL MISTER CATBERT.
"IN ORDER TO REDUCE OUR JANITORIAL EXPENSES..."
THAT'S A PHRASE YOU DON'T WANT TO SEE.
"EVERY ENGINEER WILL BE REQUIRED TO STRAP A BROOM TO HIS OR HER..."
1/21/96
© 1996 United Feature Syndicate, Inc.(NYC)
"...BUTTOCKS."
ON THE POSITIVE SIDE, MARKETING INVITES US TO A LOT MORE MEETINGS NOW.
FIVE MINUTES; WE'RE STILL EATING COOKIES.

S. Adams
1/22/96 © 1996 United Feature Syndicate, Inc.(NYC)

S. Adams
1/23/96 © 1996 United Feature Syndicate, Inc.(NYC)

S. Adams
1/24/96 © 1996 United Feature Syndicate, Inc.(NYC)

I'VE ASKED DOGBERT TO HELP US GET RID OF OUR MOST TROUBLESOME CUSTOMERS.
GRRR

TEN PERCENT OF YOUR CUSTOMERS ACCOUNT FOR NINETY PERCENT OF YOUR SERVICE COSTS. THEY MUST BE ELIMINATED.
S. Adams

IS THAT THE SAME GROUP OF CUSTOMERS WHO ACTUALLY USE OUR PRODUCT?
PLUS THE ONES WHO WERE INJURED UNPACKING IT.
1/25/96 © 1996 United Feature Syndicate, Inc.(NYC)

I'VE REDUCED YOUR SERVICE COSTS BY GIVING THE TECHNICAL-SUPPORT GROUP AN UNLISTED PHONE NUMBER.

AND A FLAW IN YOUR PRODUCT DISABLES THE CUSTOMER'S E-MAIL; THEY CAN'T EVEN WRITE TO YOU FOR HELP!
S. Adams

WHAT IF THEY ASK A FRIEND TO E-MAIL US?
PEOPLE WHO USE OUR PRODUCT DON'T HAVE FRIENDS.
REALLY? I USE IT.
1/26/96 © 1996 United Feature Syndicate, Inc.(NYC)

...BUT OUR PRIMARY VENDOR CAN'T DELIVER, SO...
I WONDER WHAT'S ON TV TONIGHT.

... SHOULD WE RISK A LAWSUIT OR BUILD A A PRODUCT THAT NOBODY ON EARTH WANTS?
DID HE ASK ME TO MAKE A CHOICE?
S. Adams

WILL IT BE A REQUEST FOR INFORMATION OR AN IMPRACTICAL SOLUTION?
LET'S DO BOTH!
1/27/96 © 1996 United Feature Syndicate, Inc.(NYC)

S. Adams 1/23/96 © 1996 United Feature Syndicate, Inc. (NYC)

S. Adams 1/29/96 © 1996 United Feature Syndicate, Inc.(NYC)

S. Adams 1/30/96 © 1996 United Feature Syndicate, Inc.(NYC)

S. Adams 1/31/96 © 1996 United Feature Syndicate, Inc.(NYC)

THANKS TO MY LEADERSHIP, THE NEW AIR TRAFFIC CONTROL SYSTEM IS DESIGNED ON TIME AND UNDER BUDGET.
S. Adams

I HAD TO CUT A FEW CORNERS. THIS BIG RADAR-LOOKING THING IS A WALL CLOCK. AND MOST OF THE BUTTONS ARE GLUED ON.

2/1/96 © 1996 United Feature Syndicate, Inc.(NYC)
IT LOOKS LIKE IT MIGHT BE UM... DANGEROUS.
GREAT... I FINISH EARLY AND WHAT DO I GET: "FEATURE CREEP."

I NEED EVERYBODY TO HELP IN THE SHIPPING DEPARTMENT TODAY.
S. Adams

EVERY PRODUCT THAT SHIPS BEFORE THE END OF THE MONTH GETS COUNTED AS REVENUE FOR THE FISCAL YEAR. UNFORTUNATELY, WE DON'T HAVE INVENTORY.

2/2/96 © 1996 United Feature Syndicate, Inc.(NYC)
SO WE'LL SHIP WHATEVER IS LYING AROUND, BOOK IT AS REVENUE AND SORT IT OUT LATER.
THIS ONE'S GETTING GUM.

HEY, WALLY! THE BOSS SENT HIS FIRST E-MAIL MESSAGE!
S. Adams

AND YOU SAID HE WASN'T BRIGHT ENOUGH TO FIGURE OUT HOW TO USE E-MAIL!
WHAT'S HIS MESSAGE?

2/3/96 © 1996 United Feature Syndicate, Inc.(NYC)
"I FORGOT MY WATCH. DOES ANYBODY KNOW WHAT TIME IT IS?"
TIME TO CHANGE JOBS.

I'LL NEVER UNDERSTAND WHAT YOU DO FOR A LIVING.
I TOLD YOU I'M AN ENGINEER, MOM.
SO YOU SAY. BUT YOU ALSO SAY YOU SPEND ALL DAY IN MEETINGS. WHEN DO YOU DO ANY ENGINEERING?
S. Adams
GOOD POINT. LET'S JUST SAY I'M WHAT THE EXPERTS CALL A "KNOWLEDGE WORKER."
WHICH EXPERTS CALL IT THAT?
I DON'T KNOW.
WHAT'S THE NAME OF THE PRODUCT YOU'RE WORKING ON?
I DON'T KNOW WHAT THE ACRONYM STANDS FOR...
2/4/96 © 1996 United Feature Syndicate, Inc. (NYC)
WHAT KIND OF MARKET PENETRATION AND RETURN ON INVESTMENT DO YOU EXPECT?
UM... I DON'T KNOW...
OH, DEAR...
WELL, I'M SURE YOU'RE VERY PUNCTUAL.
ASK ME ANOTHER QUESTION!! C'MON...
WHY DO THEY CALL YOU A "KNOWLEDGE WORKER"?

I HAVE DISCOVERED THE CAUSE OF YOUR PROJECT DELAYS.

SOMEBODY IN THIS ROOM IS A PIECE OF DEADWOOD PRETENDING TO BE A CONTRIBUTOR!
S.Adams

IT IS YOU!
HEY, I MADE SOME CALLS AND I'M WAITING FOR INFORMATION!
2/5/96 © 1996 United Feature Syndicate, Inc.(NYC)

ALICE, YOU'VE GOT TO LOCK UP THESE PROPRIETARY DOCUMENTS YOU HAVE IN YOUR CUBICLE.

IF OUR COMPETITORS SEE OUR PLANS, IT COULD BE VERY DANGEROUS.
FOR US OR FOR THEM?
S.Adams

THE COMPETITORS
OOH! LOOK! THEY'RE PLANNING TO "UTILIZE SYNERGY." WE'RE IN TROUBLE NOW!
HA HA HA
STOP! YOU'RE KILLING ME!!
2/6/96© 1996 United Feature Syndicate, Inc.(NYC)

WHY IS IT THAT THE PEOPLE WITH THE LEAST NEED FOR STORAGE SPACE HAVE THE BIGGEST OFFICES?

I KNOW! YOU'RE USING YOUR OFFICE AS KIND OF A LIVING MONUMENT TO INEFFICIENCY!
S.Adams

IS THIS BECAUSE I WOULDN'T LET YOU GET A FILE CABINET?
WHERE WOULD I PUT IT? MY CUBICLE IS FULL OF STACKS OF PROPRIETARY DOCUMENTS.
2/7/96 © 1996 United Feature Syndicate, Inc.(NYC)

2/8/96 © 1996 United Feature Syndicate, Inc.(NYC)

2/9/96 © 1996 United Feature Syndicate, Inc.(NYC)

2/10/96 © 1996 United Feature Syndicate, Inc.

SIMPLE MOLECULES COMBINE TO MAKE POWERFUL CHEMICALS...
SIMPLE CELLS COMBINE TO MAKE POWERFUL LIFE-FORMS.
S Adams
SIMPLE ELECTRONICS COMBINE TO MAKE POWERFUL COMPUTERS.
LOGICALLY, ALL THINGS ARE CREATED BY A COMBINATION OF SIMPLER, LESS CAPABLE COMPONENTS.
THEREFORE, A SUPREME BEING MUST BE OUR FUTURE, NOT OUR ORIGIN!
© 1996 United Feature Syndicate, Inc. (NYC)
WHAT IF "GOD" IS THE CONSCIOUSNESS THAT WILL BE CREATED WHEN ENOUGH OF US ARE CONNECTED BY THE INTERNET?!!
THAT WOULD CERTAINLY LIMIT THE TYPES OF FILES I DOWNLOAD.
I WONDER WHAT IT WOULD DO TO RESPONSE TIMES.
IT'S SO NICE TO SPEND TIME ALONE WITH MY THOUGHTS.
MY WEB BROWSER WOULD FLY!

CATBERT THE EVIL HUMAN RESOURCES DIRECTOR
THE EMPLOYEES HAVE TOO MUCH TIME OFF. IT MUST BE STOPPED.
S.Adams
I SUMMON THE DEMONS OF DARKNESS TO ASSIST ME!!!
2/14/96 © 1996 United Feature Syndicate, Inc.(NYC)
...ELIMINATE SICK DAYS. MAKE THEM USE VACATION DAYS WHEN THEY'RE ILL. CALL IT A "TIME BANK."
IT'S PLAYFUL... IT'S CRUEL... I LIKE IT.
I KNOW I SHOULD BE OFF TORMENTING PEOPLE...
S.Adams
BUT I CAN'T PRY MYSELF AWAY FROM THIS MOST EXCELLENT BUTT-WARMING DEVICE.
2/13/96 © 1996 United Feature Syndicate, Inc.(NYC)
IT'S PROBABLY BECAUSE OF THE HYPE, BUT I'M THINKING THIS WOULD BE EVEN BETTER WITH "WINDOWS 95."
AS A CO-OP EMPLOYEE, YOU CAN'T EXPECT THE SAME LUSH CUBICLE ENVIRONMENT THAT THE REGULAR EMPLOYEES ENJOY.
S.Adams
YOU'LL BE SHARING THIS CUBICLE WITH OUR OTHER CO-OPS.
2/14/96 © 1996 United Feature Syndicate, Inc.(NYC)
I HEARD THAT THE NEW CO-OP ONLY LASTED ONE DAY.
HE DIDN'T FIT IN.

HERE'S THE REVISED STANDARD EMPLOYMENT AGREEMENT. SIGN IT OR BE FIRED.
S.Adams

"THIS AGREEMENT IS BETWEEN THE COMPANY (HEREAFTER REFERRED TO AS 'THE ONLY COMPANY THAT WOULD EVER HIRE YOU') AND YOU (HEREAFTER CALLED 'PUDDING HEAD')."

IT SEEMS TO HAVE A BIT OF ATTITUDE.
OUR LAWYERS TURNED ON US. I SUSPECT RABIES.
2/15/96 © 1996 United Feature Syndicate, Inc.(NYC)

I CAN'T BELIEVE THEY EXPECT US TO SIGN THESE NEW EMPLOYMENT AGREEMENT FORMS.
S.Adams

ACCORDING TO THIS, ANYTHING WE EVEN THINK OF BECOMES THE COMPANY'S PROPERTY. I'M SURPRISED THEY DON'T CLAIM OUR FIRSTBORN SONS!

WHAT DO YOU SUPPOSE IT MEANS WHEN THEY COPYRIGHT OUR "DNA AND ALL DERIVATIVE WORKS"?
THEY'D MAKE AN EXCEPTION FOR YOU.
2/16/96 © 1996 United Feature Syndicate, Inc.(NYC)

LOOK AT THE AGREEMENT MY COMPANY IS FORCING US TO SIGN. THEY CLAIM THE RIGHTS TO ANY IDEA AN EMPLOYEE EVER HAS.
S.Adams

NO PROBLEM. JUST RETYPE IT WITH A FEW STRATEGIC OMISSIONS AND SIGN IT. THEY CAN'T PROOFREAD EVERY ONE.

WOULDN'T THAT BE DISHONEST?
MAYBE YOU COULD JUST SHOW THEM SOME OF YOUR IDEAS AND THEY'D GRANT A WAIVER.
2/17/96 © 1996 United Feature Syndicate, Inc.(NYC)

HERE'S MY PROJECT TIME LINE.
THE "WORK" PORTION WILL TAKE ONE WEEK.
WORK
1 WEEK
I'LL SPEND THREE WEEKS MEETING WITH PEOPLE WHOM YOU SEND TO ME BECAUSE YOU DON'T FEEL LIKE TALKING TO THEM YOURSELF.
3 WEEKS
I'LL SPEND EIGHT WEEKS GETTING COMPETITIVE BIDS FROM COMPANIES THAT I KNOW I WON'T SELECT.
... SIX WEEKS TO GET THE WISDOM AND APPROVAL OF EXECUTIVES WHO ARE TOO BUSY TO UNDERSTAND THE ISSUES.
© 1996 United Feature Syndicate, Inc. (NYC)
2/19/96
DURING THAT TIME YOU WILL RANDOMLY REORGANIZE THE DEPARTMENT AND CUT MY FUNDING.
IN THE FINAL PHASE I LEAP TO MY DEATH, A BITTER AND BROKEN SHELL OF A MAN.
EEEE!!!
IS THERE SOME SORT OF MANAGER THING I SHOULD BE DOING NOW?
IF I TIME MY LEAP RIGHT YOU'LL JUST BE LEAVING THE BUILDING.
S. Adams

THIS 3-D COLORED PIE CHART SHOWS AN UNEXPLAINED RISE IN EXPENSES.
?

YOU EACH GET A BINDER OF COLORED PIE CHARTS SO YOU CAN HELP FIND THE CAUSE OF OUR RISING EXPENSES.
S.Adams

HOW MUCH DO COLOR COPIES COST?
I THINK I SEE IT!
IT'S NOT THE "MAGIC EYE," DOOFUS.
2/19/96 © 1996 United Feature Syndicate, Inc.(NYC)

I MOVED OUR SOFTWARE DEVELOPMENT WORK TO THE IMPOVERISHED NATION OF ELBONIA.

I'M BRILLIANT. THEY WRITE HIGH-QUALITY CODE FOR SIX CENTS A DAY! THERE'S NO RISK!
RED ALERT!
S.Adams

ELBONIA
TOMORROW, YOU BE THE COMPUTER.
2/20/96 © 1996 United Feature Syndicate, Inc.(NYC)

I HEARD THAT OUR SOFTWARE DEVELOPMENT WORK HAS BEEN MOVED TO THE TINY NATION OF ELBONIA.
THINGS CAN'T GET WORSE THAN THAT.

DILBERT, YOU'RE IN CHARGE OF INTEGRATING THE ELBONIAN'S SOFTWARE WITH OUR EXISTING SYSTEMS.
S.Adams

OKAY, NOW IT CAN'T GET ANY WORSE.
YOU MIGHT WANT TO GET A TUBERCULOSIS VACCINATION.
2/21/96 © 1996 United Feature Syndicate, Inc.(NYC)

SOMEWHERE IN ELBONIA
I'VE BEEN ASSIGNED TO CHECK THE SOFTWARE YOU'RE WRITING FOR US UNDER CONTRACT.
S. Adams

THE DOCUMENTATION IS WRITTEN IN OUR OWN ELBONIAN LANGUAGE.
IS THAT A PROBLEM?

2/22/96 © 1996 United Feature Syndicate, Inc.(NYC)
THAT'S BETTER THAN I'D HOPED. I WAS AFRAID NOBODY HERE KNEW HOW TO WRITE.
WRITING IS EASY. SOMEDAY WE HOPE TO READ, TOO.

BEFORE I ACCEPT THE SOFTWARE YOU WROTE UNDER CONTRACT, TELL ME WHAT DEVELOPMENT METHODOLOGY YOU USE.
S. Adams

WE HOLD VILLAGE MEETINGS TO BOAST OF OUR SKILLS AND CURSE THE DEVIL-SPAWNED END-USERS.
SOMETIMES WE JUGGLE.

2/23/96 © 1996 United Feature Syndicate, Inc.(NYC)
AT THE LAST MINUTE WE SLAM OUT SOME CODE AND GO ROLLER SKATING.
I WOULD FIND THIS HUMOROUS IF NOT FOR THE PIG ON MY BACK.

YOU SAVED ONE MILLION DOLLARS BY HAVING PROGRAMMERS IN ELBONIA WRITE SOFTWARE FOR US.
$
S. Adams

BUT WE WASTED FOUR MILLION DOLLARS TRYING TO DEBUG THE SOFTWARE.
$

2/24/96 © 1996 United Feature Syndicate, Inc.(NYC)
AND THE ENTIRE STAFF OF OUR QUALITY ASSURANCE GROUP QUIT TO BECOME MIMES.
LET'S BLAME THE MIMES; THEY WON'T TALK.

I'M EMBARRASSED TO WORK AT MY COMPANY, DOGBERT.
WE CAN'T EVEN PAY A SIMPLE INVOICE IN LESS THAN SIX MONTHS.
S. Adams
"FIRST IT COMES TO OUR MAIL ROOM FOR AGING."
DO WE LIKE DILBERT?
BAD HAIRCUT. PENALTY BOX.
PENALTY BOX
"MONTHS LATER IT GETS TO OUR DEPARTMENT SECRETARY."
IT'S URGENT.
I'LL START IGNORING IT IMMEDIATELY.
"EVENTUALLY MY BOSS GETS IT. HE USES IT TO DEMONSTRATE HIS INABILITY TO GRASP THE CONCEPT OF TIME."
LET'S GET SOME MORE BIDS.
THAT WAS THE PAST. THIS IS THE PRESENT.
© 1998 United Feature Syndicate, Inc.(NYC)
2/25/96
"IF IT MAKES IT TO THE ACCOUNTS PAYABLE GROUP, IT WILL BE EATEN BY TROLLS."
NO, THANKS. I'M FULL.
JUST A TASTE.
HOW WOULD YOU PROTECT YOUR REPUTATION IF YOU WERE ASSOCIATED WITH SOMETHING SO PATHETIC?
I'D TELL EVERYBODY THAT THE DOOFY GUY IS MY BUTLER.
HYPOTHETICALLY.

I HATE MY SHIRTS. EACH ONE HAS EITHER A STAIN OR A MISSING BUTTON.
S.Adams

THEY SAY ENGINEERS ARE NOT CONCERNED WITH FASHION, BUT THAT'S NOT FAIR.

WHICH STAIN GOES WITH THIS TIE?
DEFINITELY THE MARINARA.
2/26/96 © 1996 United Feature Syndicate, Inc.(NYC)

I JUST GOT OUR CONSULTANT'S REPORT. HE'S IDENTIFIED OUR BIGGEST PROBLEM.
S.Adams

I RECOMMEND THAT WE BUILD A TRACKING DATABASE.
WE CAN PUT IT ON THE NETWORK.
2/27/96 © 1996 United Feature Syndicate, Inc.(NYC)

WOULD YOU LIKE TO HEAR WHAT THE PROBLEM IS FIRST?
I HATE TO DWELL ON THE NEGATIVE.
WE LIKE DATABASES.

YOU HAVEN'T HEARD WHAT THE PROBLEM IS YET; HOW CAN YOU RECOMMEND BUILDING A DATABASE TO SOLVE IT??
S.Adams

WE ALWAYS BUILD A DATABASE.
AND WE'LL NEED COFFEE MUGS FOR THE PROJECT TEAM.
2/29/96 © 1996 United Feature Syndicate, Inc.(NYC)

THE PROBLEM IS THAT WE HAVE POOR PROCESSES.
THAT COULD BE THE SLOGAN ON OUR MUGS!

DOGBERT, I NEED YOU TO FACILITATE SOME MEETINGS.
WHAT KIND OF MEETINGS?
S.Adams

WE'RE CREATING A PROCESS TO FIX OUR PRODUCT DEVELOPMENT PROCESS. BUT FIRST WE'RE HAVING SOME PREPLANNING MEETINGS...

2/29/96 © 1996 United Feature Syndicate, Inc.(NYC)
...TO DECIDE ON A PROJECT NAME.
HOW ABOUT "DEATH SPIRAL"?

I'VE BEEN ASKED TO FACILITATE THIS MEETING. I ALONE WILL DETERMINE WHO CAN SPEAK.
S.Adams

I'D LIKE TO BEGIN WITH A RAW DISPLAY OF MY POWER. YOU MAY NOT SPEAK.

3/1/96 © 1996 United Feature Syndicate, Inc.(NYC)
HEY, WALLY... DID YOU EVER HEAR OF A THING CALLED EXERCISE?

I THINK YOU'LL AGREE THAT THIS MEETING WENT SMOOTHLY WITH ME AS FACILITATOR.
S.Adams

THE BREAKTHROUGH WAS WHEN I REALIZED I WAS THE ONLY ONE HERE WITH ANYTHING VALUABLE TO SAY.

3/2/96 © 1996 United Feature Syndicate, Inc.(NYC)
LET'S HAVE A MOMENT OF SILENCE TO HONOR ME FOR MY BRILLIANT WORK DESPITE BEING SURROUNDED BY DOLTS.

I WANT YOU TO INTERVIEW THE NEW CANDIDATE FOR ENGINEERING. DON'T REVEAL ANY UGLY TRUTHS.
AT THIS COMPANY WE'RE DEDICATED TO THE PRINCIPLE OF EMPLOYEE EMPOWERMENT, JENNIFER.
THE "PRINCIPLE OF EMPLOYEE EMPOWERMENT"?
UH-OH.
WHY WOULD YOU HAVE A SPECIAL PHRASE FOR SOMETHING LIKE THAT?
IF YOU COULD REALLY MAKE DECISIONS ON YOUR OWN IT WOULD NEVER OCCUR TO YOU TO INVENT A PHRASE FOR IT.
© 1996 United Feature Syndicate, Inc.(NYC)
3/3/96
MY SHIELDS ARE DOWN... A HULL BREACH IS IMMINENT...
JUST DON'T TELL ME YOU HAVE "QUALITY TEAMS".
RUN FOR IT, JENNIFER!!! IT'S TOO LATE FOR ME BUT YOU CAN SAVE YOURSELF!!! RUN!!!
WHOA! HULL BREACH. ANY SURVIVORS?
ONE. I HAD TO JETTISON MY DIGNITY BUT SHE MADE IT TO THE ESCAPE POD.
S. Adams

ADD AN EXECUTIVE SUMMARY TO THE APPROVAL PAGE.

KEEP IT SIMPLE. OUR EXECUTIVES DON'T UNDERSTAND AS MUCH ABOUT TECHNOLOGY AS I DO.
S. Adams

HOW COULD THEY KNOW LESS THAN YOU DO? YOU HAVEN'T FIGURED OUT HOW TO MAKE YOUR CAR GO UPHILL.
WRONG; I GOT AAA ROAD SERVICE.
3/4/96 © 1996 United Feature Syndicate, Inc.(NYC)

I HAVE TO TURN THIS FIFTY-PAGE PROPOSAL INTO A ONE-PARAGRAPH EXECUTIVE SUMMARY FOR OUR CEO. IT'S IMPOSSIBLE.
SIMPLE.

HOW ABOUT "GIVE US THREE MILLION DOLLARS SO WE CAN BUY COOL TECHNOLOGY, PUMP UP OUR RÉSUMÉS AND ESCAPE THIS FESTERING BOIL YOU CALL A COMPANY"?
S. Adams

I FEEL OBLIGATED TO SAY SOMETHING ABOUT OUR CUSTOMERS.
HOW ABOUT "I'M GLAD I'M NOT ONE OF THEM."
3/5/96 © 1996 United Feature Syndicate, Inc.(NYC)

COULD YOU DO A DEMO OF THE NEW PRODUCT FOR OUR VP NEXT WEEK?

WELL... THAT WOULD DELAY THE SHIP DATE, LOWER MORALE AND CREATE AN UNENDING DEMAND FOR MORE UNPRODUCTIVE DEMOS...
S. Adams

LOGICALLY, SINCE YOUR OBJECTIVE IS TO SHOW THAT WE'RE DOING VALUABLE WORK...
AND WE'LL NEED A BANNER THAT SAYS "QUALITY."
3/6/96 © 1996 United Feature Syndicate, Inc.(NYC)

WE HAD TO CUT SOME CORNERS TO GET THE DEMO READY THIS SOON.
S.Adams

WALLY IS UNDER THE TABLE. HE'LL PRETEND TO BE THE 3-D INTERFACE THAT WE COULD BUILD IF WE WEREN'T DOING USELESS DEMOS.

HE'S A LITTLE FUZZY. CAN YOU ADJUST IT?
TRY THE ELECTRIC SHAVER.
3/7/96 © 1996 United Feature Syndicate, Inc.(NYC)

OUR NEW VP IS COMING. IS THE DEMO OF OUR HOLOGRAPHIC INTERFACE READY?

EVERYTHING SHOULD BE FINE... UNLESS WE'RE SUDDENLY VISITED BY THE DARK ANGEL OF PRODUCT DEMOS...
S.Adams

HELLO-O-O, WALLY. DID SOMEBODY SAY "DEMO"?
I'M DILBERT, LOYAL PEON.
3/8/96 © 1996 United Feature Syndicate, Inc.(NYC)

WE PLANNED A DAZZLING DEMO FOR YOU, BUT AS YOU CAN SEE WE'RE BEING VISITED BY THE DARK ANGEL OF DEMOS.

THE DEMO IS A SHAM. THEIR PROJECT IS DOOMED. CUT THEIR FUNDING BEFORE YOUR NAME IS ASSOCIATED WITH IT.
S.Adams

THE WORST IS OVER.
LOOK AT SOME OF THE PICTURES THE "BOYS" STORE ON THE FILE SERVER...
3/9/96 © 1996 United Feature Syndicate, Inc.(NYC)

S. Adams
3/10/96 © 1996 United Feature Syndicate, Inc.(NYC)

WALLY AND I CAME UP WITH A GREAT NEW PRODUCT IDEA!
INSPIRATION ALERT IN EFFECT!!
DANGER! NEW IDEA!
S.Adams
3/11/96 © 1996 United Feature Syndicate, Inc.(NYC)
STATE YOUR IDEA NOW
CRUSH-O-MATIC
UM, YOU TELL HIM.

IF THIS COMPANY WON'T USE OUR PRODUCT IDEA LET'S QUIT AND START OUR OWN BUSINESS!
S.Adams
WHY QUIT? WE CAN RUN OUR NEW COMPANY FROM OUR CUBICLES AND GET PAID TOO.
3/12/96 © 1996 United Feature Syndicate, Inc.(NYC)
WOULDN'T THAT BE IMMORAL?
THAT'S ONLY AN ISSUE FOR PEOPLE WHO AREN'T ALREADY IN HELL.

IT HAS COME TO MY ATTENTION THAT SOME EMPLOYEES ARE RUNNING SIDE BUSINESSES FROM THEIR CUBICLES.
REALLY??
S.Adams
I DON'T WANT TO SEE ANY SIGNS OF THAT IN MY DEPARTMENT.
FAIR ENOUGH.
3/13/96 © 1996 United Feature Syndicate, Inc.(NYC)
SOFTWARE OUTLET
SALE
PALMS READ $25
SHOE WORLD
WHAT ABOUT "YELLOW PAGES" ADS?
WALBERT INC.

RATBERT, WE'D LIKE YOU TO BE THE DIRECTOR OF MARKETING FOR THE COMPANY WE'RE STARTING.
OKAY! WHAT DO I DO?
S. Adams

BE AS ANNOYING AND ILLOGICAL AS YOU CAN. WE'LL WHACK YOU IN THE HEAD WITH BALLED-UP SOCKS TO MAKE YOU SHUT UP.

IT'S DEFINITELY BETTER TO BE AN OWNER THAN AN EMPLOYEE.
LET'S LINK HIS SALARY TO EARNINGS! HEE HEE!
3/4/96 © 1996 United Feature Syndicate, Inc. (NYC)

THE BUSINESS PLAN FOR YOUR START-UP IS IDIOTIC BUT I'M GOING TO PROVIDE THE VENTURE CAPITAL FUNDING ANYWAY.
S. Adams

WE'LL GENERATE LOTS OF MEDIA HYPE, GO PUBLIC AND MAKE MILLIONS BY SHAFTING GREEDY AND IGNORANT INVESTORS.

THE LATIN WORD FOR "CLOSE YOUR EYES AND OPEN YOUR MOUTH" IS "PROSPECTUS."
THIS IS EXACTLY WHY I'M AFRAID OF DOGS.
3/5/96 © 1996 United Feature Syndicate, Inc. (NYC)

WALLY AND I STARTED OUR OWN COMPANY. WE'RE SELLING THE PRODUCT THAT YOU SAID NOBODY WANTS.
SOON WE WILL BE RICH.
S. Adams

WE DO OUR VICTORY JIG IN YOUR FACE.
BA-BUM

WHEN HE SHOWED YOU YOUR EMPLOYMENT AGREEMENT - WHERE YOU GAVE ALL PATENT RIGHTS TO THIS COMPANY - WHAT PART OF THE JIG WERE YOU DOING?
TURBO MOONING.
SOB
3/16/96 © 1996 United Feature Syndicate, Inc. (NYC)

I HAVE AN ETHICAL QUESTION, DOGBERT.
I'M HERE TO HELP.
IS IT BETTER TO GIVE CUSTOMERS A LOW QUALITY PRODUCT IN A TIMELY FASHION...
S. Adams
OR IS IT BETTER TO LIE ABOUT PRODUCT AVAILABILITY UNTIL THE BUGS ARE FIXED?
I WILL NEED MY ASSISTANT, RATBERT, TO ADDRESS YOUR ETHICAL QUESTION.
SNAP
LET'S SAY RATBERT IS A TRUSTING AND INNOCENT CUSTOMER.
© 1996 United Feature Syndicate, Inc. (NYC)
3/17/96
SUPPOSE SOMEBODY ABUSES HIS TRUST LIKE THIS...
SMACK
HOW DOES THIS RELATE TO MY SITUATION?
TO BE HONEST, I WASN'T LISTENING TO YOU.

HEY, EVERYBODY. MEET OUR NEW INTERN, ASOK.

I HOPE THIS ONE'S STURDIER THAN THE LAST ONE.
S.Adams

MY STAPLE REMOVER IS BROKEN. SOMEBODY TOSS THAT INTERN TO ME!
3/18/96 © 1996 United Feature Syndicate, Inc.(NYC)

ASOK THE INTERN
AS AN INTERN, YOUR ASSIGNMENTS WON'T BE AS GLAMOROUS AS MINE, BUT YOU'LL GAIN EXPERIENCE.

DILBERT, I NEED A STATUS REPORT ON THE MOUSE PAD INVENTORY.
S.Adams

SEE? MY ASSIGNMENT HAS THE WORD "STATUS" BUILT RIGHT IN.
DANGER! ALERT!
3/19/96 © 1996 United Feature Syndicate, Inc.(NYC)

ASOK THE INTERN
ASOK, COME QUICKLY! IT'S AN EMERGENCY!

YOU MUST CRAWL THROUGH THE JEFFRIES TUBE AND SHUT DOWN THE FURNACE BEFORE IT FRIES US ALL!
S.Adams

TODAY YOUNG ASOK LEARNS THAT LIFE IS NOT LIKE "STAR TREK."
I'M STUCK.
SPANK THE INTERN 50¢
3/20/96 © 1996 United Feature Syndicate, Inc.(NYC)

I WANT EVERYONE TO PREPARE A PRESENTATION FOR THE EXECUTIVE REVIEW BOARD. URGENT.
S. Adams
WHAT'S THAT SMELL? YES!!! ...IT'S THE SCENT OF UNNECESSARY WORK FOR A MEETING THAT WILL BE CANCELED.
SNIFF SNIFF
3/21/96 © 1996 United Feature Syndicate, Inc.(NYC)
DID YOU SMELL THE UNNECESSARY WORK? WE CAN IGNORE IT!
IT'S LIKE POPCORN FOR THE SOUL.
URGENT

WHY AREN'T YOU SLAVING AWAY, PREPARING FOR THE EXECUTIVE REVIEW BOARD MEETING?
S. Adams
I HAVE THE MALE "WORK AVOIDANCE CHROMOSOME." I CAN DETECT UNNECESSARY WORK, THEREBY AVOIDING IT.
3/22/96 © 1996 United Feature Syndicate, Inc.(NYC)
WE ALL HAVE TO BE READY TO PRESENT SOMETHING!
COULD YOU HOLD IT DOWN? I'M TRYING TO SLEEP.

I DON'T BELIEVE MEN HAVE A SPECIAL CHROMOSOME TO TELL THEM WHICH ASSIGNMENTS ARE A WASTE OF TIME.
WE DO.
S. Adams
I WILL TEST THE THEORY ON YOUNG ASOK THE INTERN.
MMM... THE SWEET SMELL OF UNNECESSARY WORK.
3/23/96 © 1996 United Feature Syndicate, Inc.(NYC)
MAYBE MEN ARE MORE PERCEPTIVE THAN YOU'D THINK.
SHE'S AROUSED. I'LL MAKE MY MOVE.

HERE'S THE ANALYSIS YOU ASKED FOR... I WORKED ALL NIGHT.
BUT YOU SAID THIS WAS VITAL FOR YOUR MEETING TODAY SO I KNOW IT WAS WORTH THE EFFORT.
S Adams
THIS IS EXCELLENT WORK, ALICE.
A RARE COMPLIMENT; IT WAS ALL WORTH-WHILE.
MMM
I'LL USE IT AS BACKUP MATERIAL.
BACKUP?!! NOBODY LOOKS AT BACKUP MATERIAL!
© 1996 United Feature Syndicate, Inc.(NYC)
3/24/96
I'M GOING TO GRAB YOUR POINTY HAIR, YANK YOU OUT OF THAT CHEAP SUIT AND FLING YOUR NAKED BODY DOWN THE HALL.
SHE'S ALWAYS IRRITABLE THE WEEK BEFORE HER PERFORMANCE REVIEW CYCLE.
HER DISTANCE IMPROVED THIS YEAR.
OW

AT LONG LAST OUR PRODUCT IS COMPLETE. IT SHIPS TOMORROW.

THAT'S TERRIFIC. I ONLY HAVE A FEW ADDITIONAL FEATURES TO ADD AND THE MARKETING DEPARTMENT WILL BE HAPPY.
OKAY
S. Adams

I BELIEVE THAT OUR CUSTOMERS WANT HARDWARE, NOT SOFTWARE.
IT'S TIMES LIKE THIS I WISH I WERE A PSYCHOPATH.
YOU'RE NOT?
3/25/96 © 1996 United Feature Syndicate, Inc.(NYC)

I WANT YOU THREE TO WRITE THE DEPARTMENT NEWSLETTER. IT'S AN IMPORTANT, HIGH-PROFILE ASSIGNMENT.

I AM AN EXPERIENCED TECHNICAL WRITER. YOU HAVE PLACED ME ON A PROJECT WITH AN INTERN AND A RODENT.
S. Adams

MY NEXT RAISE WILL DEPEND ON THEIR PERFORMANCE.
I'LL DO THE SPORTS PAGE!
I'LL BE THE TOPLESS MODEL ON PAGE TWO.
3/26/96 © 1996 United Feature Syndicate, Inc.(NYC)

LET'S GET ONE THING STRAIGHT BEFORE WE START WRITING THE DEPARTMENT NEWSLETTER...

I'M AN EXPERIENCED TECHNICAL WRITER. YOU ARE AN INTERN AND A RAT, RESPECTIVELY. THEREFORE I WILL BE THE EDITOR.
S. Adams

I HAVE NO SKILLS WHATSOEVER. THEREFORE I'LL BE EXECUTIVE EDITOR.
IS "PUBLISHER" TAKEN?
3/27/96 © 1996 United Feature Syndicate, Inc.(NYC)

AT THE RISK OF DYING FROM BOREDOM, I MUST INTERVIEW YOU FOR THE DEPARTMENT NEWSLETTER.
LET ME GIVE YOU SOME BACKGROUND BEFORE I TALK ABOUT MY PROJECT...
S. Adams
"THE PROJECT IS GOOD," QUIPPED THE ENGINEER.
...SO THERE I AM IN MY MOM'S FALLOPIAN TUBE...
3/29/96 © 1996 United Feature Syndicate, Inc.(NYC)

WALLY, I'M HOPING YOU'LL AGREE TO WRITE ABOUT YOUR PROJECT FOR THE NEWSLETTER...
S. Adams
AND IN THE GRAND TRADITION OF ENGINEERING, I EXPECT YOU'LL GIVE THIS THE LOWEST PRIORITY, THUS MAKING ME DESPISE YOU.
3/29/96 © 1996 United Feature Syndicate, Inc.(NYC)
SO... ARE YOU SAYING YOU DON'T DESPISE ME NOW?
WE ARE NOT HAVING A "MOMENT" HERE!

PERFORMANCE REVIEW
YOUR MAIN ACCOMPLISHMENT WAS THE DEPARTMENT NEWSLETTER WHICH WAS BOTH UNINTERESTING AND UNIMPORTANT. YOU GET NO RAISE.
S. Adams
THE NEWSLETTER WAS YOUR IDEA, AND IT'S BORING BECAUSE MOST OF THE ARTICLES ARE CONTRIBUTED BY MY IDIOTIC COWORKERS.
3/30/96 © 1996 United Feature Syndicate, Inc.(NYC)
YOU DON'T SEEM TO UNDERSTAND THE VALUE OF TEAMWORK.
I UNDERSTAND ITS VALUE; IT JUST COST ME A TWO-PERCENT RAISE.

IT'S MY HONOR TO PRESENT THIS SPECIAL BONUS CHECK TO BARRY.
THAT'S YOU.
MY NAME IS BARRY??
THIS IS FOR WORKING HUNDREDS OF HOURS OF OVER-TIME.
WHILE YOU QUITTERS WERE GOING HOME BY 9 PM EVERY NIGHT...
BARRY REMAINED AT WORK STARING AT HIS COMPUTER FOR HOURS.
IT'S IMPORTANT TO RECOGNIZE EXTRA EFFORT.
SADLY, THAT'S THE END OF THE SPECIAL BONUS BUDGET FOR THE YEAR.
BURP
IN RETROSPECT, I SHOULDN'T HAVE TOLD BARRY THAT HIS SCREEN SAVER IS AN EPIC MINI-SERIES.
© 1996 United Feature Syndicate, Inc.(NY©)
S Adams
3/31/96

IN AN EFFORT TO BOOST SALES, LAPTOP COMPUTERS HAVE BEEN GIVEN TO EVERY MEMBER OF THE SALES FORCE.
THAT COULD BE A PROBLEM, GIVEN THE RECENT CUTS TO THE TRAINING BUDGET.
MEANWHILE, IN THE FIELD
AND IF YOU ORDER TODAY, I'LL THROW IN THIS RECTANGULAR PLASTIC THING.
S.Adams
4/1/96 © 1996 United Feature Syndicate, Inc.(NYC)

I WISH I HAD AN IVY LEAGUE DEGREE SO I COULD BE PROMOTED TO VICE PRESIDENT.
YOU DON'T NEED ONE.
IT'S IMPOSSIBLE TO BE A VICE PRESIDENT WITHOUT ONE.
I'LL BET $100 I CAN TURN A RAT INTO A VICE PRESIDENT.
THAT WAS GOOD, BUT TRY SAYING IT AS THOUGH YOUR SOUL JUST ABANDONED YOUR BODY.
"WE'VE REORGANIZED TO FOCUS ON OUR CORE COMPETENCY."
S.Adams
4/2/96 © 1996 United Feature Syndicate, Inc.(NYC)

REMEMBER EVERYTHING I TAUGHT YOU, RATBERT. IF YOU CAN PASS YOURSELF OFF AS A CORPORATE VICE PRESIDENT, I'LL WIN MY BET.
YO, HEADCOUNT! IF YOU HAVE ANY ISSUES, PUT TOGETHER AN ACTION PLAN. OUR PEOPLE ARE THE BEST. DON'T SPEND MONEY.
DO YOU THINK HE'S REALLY A VICE PRESIDENT?
MAYBE. BUT I'M NOT READY TO RULE OUT "ANNOYING RODENT" YET.
QUALITY.
S.Adams
4/3/96 © 1996 United Feature Syndicate, Inc.(NYC)

MISTER RATBERT, I DON'T THINK I CAN HIRE A RAT TO BE OUR VICE PRESIDENT OF MARKETING. YOU NEED EXPERIENCE IN THE TECHNOLOGY INDUSTRY.

I SPENT A WEEK IN A DUMPSTER AT PROCTER AND GAMBLE.
S. Adams

CLOSE ENOUGH! WELCOME TO THE TEAM!
I'LL BRING SOME CRONIES WITH ME. THEY'RE FLIES.
4/4/96 © 1996 United Feature Syndicate, Inc.(NYC)

I HAD YEARS OF VALUABLE EXPERIENCE AS A RODENT BEFORE I BECAME VICE PRESIDENT OF MARKETING.

MY MARKETING PLAN IS SIMPLE. EACH OF YOU WILL CLING TO THE LEG OF A TECHNOLOGY COLUMNIST UNTIL WE GET SOME GOOD PRESS.
S. Adams

IT LOOKS LIKE YOU'RE FULL.
YOU CAN CLING TO THE CAT UNTIL A SPACE OPENS.
4/5/96 © 1996 United Feature Syndicate, Inc.(NYC)

I QUIT MY JOB AS VICE PRESIDENT OF MARKETING...

I WAS LOSING MY SCRUPLES... BECOMING UNSCRUPULOUS. YES, I LEARNED A VALUABLE LESSON ABOUT SCRUPLES.
S. Adams

AND THAT LESSON WOULD BE?
IT'S FUN TO SAY "SCRUPLES."
4/6/96 © 1996 United Feature Syndicate, Inc.(NYC)

GO HOME, DILBERT. RELAX! YOU'RE WORKING TOO HARD!
YOU TOLD ME TO FINISH THIS BY TOMORROW. YOU SAID IT'S URGENT.
S Adams
RELAX! GO HOME! SHOO!
SUDDENLY DILBERT IS SUCKED INTO THE "BOSS ZONE" WHERE TIME AND LOGIC DO NOT APPLY.
HOW CAN I RELAX AND DO URGENT WORK AT THE SAME TIME?
4/7/96 © 1996 United Feature Syndicate, Inc.
WORK SMARTER, NOT HARDER.
AAEEIT!!
MERCIFULLY, THE ANGEL OF CYNICISM APPEARS.
SLAP SOMETHING TOGETHER IN THE MORNING. HE WON'T LOOK AT IT ANYWAY.
THE INSPIRATIONAL MORAL...
FREEDOM'S JUST ANOTHER WORD FOR NOT CARING ABOUT THE QUALITY OF YOUR WORK!

THE EXECUTIVE REVIEW BOARD MEETING IS CANCELED. I HOPE YOU DIDN'T WORK TOO HARD PREPARING FOR IT.

MUST... CONTROL FIST... OF... DEATH...
UNLIKE ALICE, I SAW IT COMING AND DID NO WORK WHATSOEVER.
S.Adams

DID YOU SEE THAT COMING, NOSTRA-DAMUS?
WHAT DOES THIS DO TO HEADCOUNT?
OW
4/8/96 © 1996 United Feature Syndicate, Inc.(NYC)

STUPID MACHINE, YOU'VE TAKEN MY COINS AND WITH THEM MY SUNNY DISPOSITION.
Soda

THERE'S NOTHING LEFT TO GIVE!!! YOU'VE TAKEN IT ALL!!!
S.Adams

OKAY, YOU GOT MY DIGNITY AND MY CAREER, TOO... BUT I AM DRAWING THE LINE HERE, BUSTER!
4/9/96 © 1996 United Feature Syndicate, Inc.(NYC)

CATBERT THE H.R. DIRECTOR
THIS REPORT SAYS YOU WENT NUTS AT A VENDING MACHINE BECAUSE IT TOOK YOUR MONEY.

THE COMPANY USED TO OFFER COUNSELING IN THESE CASES. BUT WE FOUND IT WAS MORE ECONOMICAL TO APPLY THE DEATH PENALTY.
S.Adams

WHAT?! HOW IS THAT POSSIBLE?
I'M NOT SURE YET. YOU'RE TOO BIG FOR THE MICRO-WAVE OVEN...
4/10/96 © 1996 United Feature Syndicate, Inc.(NYC)

TODAY WAS A BAD DAY. FIRST THE VENDING MACHINE STOLE MY MONEY...

...AND BY THE END OF THE DAY I HAD BEEN SENTENCED TO DEATH BY THE DIRECTOR OF HUMAN RESOURCES...
S.Adams

I'VE BECOME TOTALLY DESENSITIZED TO TRAGIC NEWS!
THE EXECUTION IS SCHEDULED FOR TOMORROW. I SHOULD CALL IN SICK.
4/1/96 © 1996 United Feature Syndicate, Inc.(NYC)

DOGBERT VERSUS CATBERT
I UNDERSTAND YOU'VE SENTENCED DILBERT TO DEATH.
IS THAT A PROBLEM?

MY ASSISTANT, BOB THE DINOSAUR, WILL NOW DEMONSTRATE HOW TO GIVE A CAT A "FUR WEDGIE."
S.Adams

I'VE BEEN PARDONED. SOMEHOW THEY LOST THE PAPERWORK ORDERING MY EXECUTION.
IT PROBABLY FELL INTO A CRACK.
4/2/96 © 1996 United Feature Syndicate, Inc.(NYC)

THE INTERNAL JOB POSTINGS ARE OUT. HERE'S A JOB I'D LOVE.

" EXPERIENCE REQUIRED: THE CANDIDATE MUST BE A GUY NAMED ERIC, POT-BELLIED, NEARSIGHTED, MUST DRIVE A RED FORD BRONCO."
S.Adams

THEY MIGHT HAVE SOMEONE IN MIND ALREADY.
IF I SQUINT... AND LEAVE MY "CONTROL TOP" PANTYHOSE AT HOME...
4/3/96 © 1996 United Feature Syndicate, Inc.(NYC)

© 1996 United Feature Syndicate, Inc.

ALICE, YOU'VE BEEN WORKING EIGHTEEN HOURS A DAY. I REALIZED I MUST ADD A PERSON TO THE EFFORT.

SO I HIRED A NIGHT SHIFT MANAGER. AFTER I GO HOME AT FIVE O'CLOCK HE'LL TAKE OVER AND ASK WHY YOU'RE BEHIND SCHEDULE.
S.Adams

I LIKE MY STATUS REPORTS RENDERED IN 3-D, BUT DON'T SPEND A LOT OF TIME ON IT.
4/15/96 © 1996 United Feature Syndicate, Inc.(NYC)

THIS DOG IS SPECIALLY TRAINED TO DETECT WASTED RESOURCES.

HE'LL HELP ME FIND OUT WHY YOUR PROJECT IS BEHIND SCHEDULE EVEN AFTER ADDING ME AS MANAGER.
SNIFF SNIFF
S.Adams

WE'LL BEGIN AS SOON AS HE'S DONE PLAYING AROUND.
4/16/96 © 1996 United Feature Syndicate, Inc.(NYC)

OH MY! THIS IS SHOCKING!
WHAT?

40% OF ALL SICK DAYS TAKEN BY YOUR STAFF ARE FRIDAYS AND MONDAYS!
S.Adams

WHAT KIND OF IDIOT DO THEY THINK I AM?
NOT AN IDIOT SAVANT. THEY CAN DO MATH.
4/17/96 © 1996 United Feature Syndicate, Inc.(NYC)

IT HAS COME TO MY ATTENTION THAT 40% OF YOUR SICK DAYS ARE ON FRIDAYS AND MONDAYS. THIS IS UNACCEPTABLE.

HA HA HA!!! THAT'S A GOOD ONE!!!
S.Adams

PLEASE TELL ME HE WAS KIDDING.
WELCOME TO HELL, KID.
4/18/96 © 1996 United Feature Syndicate, Inc.(NYC)

I CAN MAKE YOUR EMPLOYEES MORE CREATIVE AND SPIRITUALLY FULFILLED.

I USE MY SPECIAL BLEND OF POETRY AND DANCE TO TOUCH THEIR SOULS.
OKAY. YOU'RE HIRED.
S.Adams

THERE ONCE WAS A DOG WITH A HAT... WHO GOT PAID TO DANCE LIKE THAT...
HEY! MY SOUL JUST HEALED!
4/19/96 © 1996 United Feature Syndicate, Inc.(NYC)

HAVE MY POEMS AND DANCES HEALED YOUR SOUL YET, ALICE? THE COMPANY CARES ABOUT YOUR TOTAL WELL BEING.
EXCUSE ME.

WE WANT MORE MONEY, NOT MORE DANCING DOGS!!! M-O-N-E-Y!!
S.Adams

SO YOU'RE SAYING THOSE PRIMAL SCREAMS ARE HEALTHY? CAN YOU TEACH ME TO DO IT?
HERE'S MY INVOICE-GO WILD.
4/20/96 © 1996 United Feature Syndicate, Inc.(NYC)

4/21/96 © 1996 United Feature Syndicate, Inc.

CATBERT, H.R. DIRECTOR
WALLY, IT MIGHT NOT SEEM FAIR THAT NEW EMPLOYEES ARE PAID MORE THAN YOU...
BUT YOU COULD ALWAYS QUIT AND THEN REAPPLY FOR YOUR OLD JOB AT A HIGHER SALARY.
S. Adams
4/22/96 © 1996 United Feature Syndicate, Inc. (NYC)
I JUST MIGHT DO THAT!!
WOULD YOU MIND RUBBING THIS CATNIP ALL OVER YOUR BODY FIRST?

SO I'M THINKING I'LL RESIGN, THEN I'LL REAPPLY FOR MY CURRENT JOB AT A HIGHER SALARY.
S. Adams
THAT'S A GOOD PLAN EXCEPT FOR THE FACT THAT YOU'RE THOROUGHLY UNQUALIFIED FOR YOUR CURRENT JOB.
4/23/96 © 1996 United Feature Syndicate, Inc. (NYC)
I NEED TO SHARE MY UNREALISTIC PLANS WITH A FRIEND WHO ISN'T AN ENGINEER.
I'M MORE OF A CO-WORKER THAN A FRIEND, PER SE.

AND THAT'S THE MARKETING PLAN. ANY COMMENTS?
S. Adams
IT APPEARS TO BE A BUNCH OF OBVIOUS GENERALITIES AND WISHFUL THINKING WITH NO APPARENT BUSINESS VALUE.
4/24/96 © 1996 United Feature Syndicate, Inc. (NYC)
MARKETING DIDN'T TURN OUT TO BE THE GLAMOUR CAREER I EXPECTED.
I CIRCLED ALL THE WORDS YOU WON'T FIND IN ANY DICTIONARY.

S. Adams
4/25/96 © 1996 United Feature Syndicate, Inc.(NYC)

S. Adams
4/26/96 © 1996 United Feature Syndicate, Inc.(NYC)

S. Adams
4/27/96 © 1996 United Feature Syndicate, Inc.(NYC)

GREAT NEWS! THE COMPANY SET A NEW RECORD FOR PROFITS!
THAT MEANS T-SHIRTS FOR EVERYONE!
S. Adams
YOU CAN CHOOSE FROM SIZES "SMALL," "PETITE" OR "ELFIN."
SHOULDN'T THESE HAVE THE COMPANY NAME OR LOGO ON THEM?
HEY, THAT'S AN IDEA FOR NEXT YEAR!
IT'S 1% COTTON, 99% "MISCELLANEOUS" AND ALL HAND-MADE BY AUTHENTIC SLAVE LABORERS.
4/28/96 © 1996 United Feature Syndicate, Inc.
THAT'S GREAT! WITH SLAVE LABOR YOU DON'T HAVE THE PROBLEM THAT THE SHIRTS MADE ON FRIDAYS AREN'T AS GOOD!
DO YOU EVER WORRY THAT OUR CAREER EXPECTATIONS HAVE GOTTEN TOO LOW?
DON'T GO THERE, ALICE.
"CASUAL DAY," HERE I COME!

CATBERT, H.R. DIRECTOR
I'VE COME TO GIVE YOU "EMPLOYEE ORIENTATION," WALLY.
BUT I'VE WORKED HERE FOR YEARS.
S. Adams

YOU STILL HAVE A GLIMMER OF HOPE. YOU'LL HAVE TO WATCH THIS MANDATORY TRAINING VIDEO.
HOPE

SO, YOU STILL HAVE HOPE...
RELAX... LET IT GO.
4/29/96 © 1996 United Feature Syndicate, Inc. (NYC)

I'M PLEASED TO REPORT ANOTHER BANNER WEEK OF ACCOMPLISHMENTS!
S. Adams

I STREAMLINED MY BUSINESS PROCESSES WHILE HONING MY PARTICIPATORY STYLE AND MY PROACTIVE ATTITUDE, ALL WHILE VALUING DIVERSITY!

YOU WATCHED THE MANDATORY TRAINING VIDEOS?
AND I LOST MY FREE WILL!
4/30/96 © 1996 United Feature Syndicate, Inc. (NYC)

I JUST WATCHED THE MANDATORY VIDEO ON SEXUAL HARASSMENT. IT WORKED!
S. Adams

IN ONLY THIRTY MINUTES, THAT VIDEO CORRECTED A BILLION YEARS OF EVOLUTION. DO SOMETHING SEXY AND WATCH ME IGNORE IT!

I PROBABLY SHOULDN'T HAVE FAST-FORWARDED THROUGH THE BORING PARTS.
5/1/96 © 1996 United Feature Syndicate, Inc. (NYC)

HERE'S YOUR PROBLEM. THE CONNECTION TO THE NETWORK IS BROKEN.

UH-OH. IT'S A "TOKEN RING" LAN. THAT MEANS THE TOKEN FELL OUT AND IT'S IN THIS ROOM SOMEPLACE.
S. Adams

YOU ARE THE WIND BENEATH MY WINGS.
I'LL WAIT A WEEK THEN TELL HIM THE TOKEN MUST BE IN THE "ETHERNET."
5/2/96 © 1996 United Feature Syndicate, Inc.(NYC)

WE'LL HAVE TO ELIMINATE A FEW STEPS IN ORDER TO HIT THE MARKET WINDOW.

I THINK WE CAN GET RID OF MARKET RESEARCH AND TECHNICAL TESTING. THEY'RE BASICALLY "OVERHEAD."
S. Adams

GONE! NOW WE'LL HIT THE WINDOW!
...LIKE A BIRD.
5/3/96 © 1996 United Feature Syndicate, Inc.(NYC)

HERE ARE MY BUDGET ESTIMATES FOR THE YEAR.

THANKS TO MANAGEMENT BUNGLING AND INDECISION, I PLAN TO USE NO CAPITAL FOR SEVERAL MONTHS FOLLOWED BY A RECKLESS YEAR-END ORGY OF ACQUISITION.
S. Adams

IS THAT WHAT YOU WERE LOOKING FOR?
TELL ME AGAIN WHAT "CAPITAL" IS.
5/4/96 © 1996 United Feature Syndicate, Inc.(NYC)

S. Adams
5/5/96 © 1996 United Feature Syndicate, Inc.

THIS WEEK I KICKED OFF THE "WALLY COMPENSATION EQUILIBRIUM PROJECT."
S.Adams

MY GOAL IS TO LOWER THE QUALITY OF MY WORK UNTIL IT IS CONSISTENT WITH MY SALARY.

5/6/96 © 1996 United Feature Syndicate, Inc.(NYC)
I HATE THE FIRST MONTH AFTER THEY SEE THEIR RAISES.
I'D GO ON, BUT I JUST ACHIEVED EQUILIBRIUM.

CATBERT, THE EVIL DIRECTOR OF HUMAN RESOURCES
WE'RE MOVING TO "CAFETERIA STYLE" BENEFITS.
S.Adams

UNDER THIS SYSTEM, IF YOU NEED HEALTH CARE, YOU WANDER THROUGH THE CAFETERIA ASKING "DOES ANYBODY KNOW WHAT THIS RED LUMP IS?"

5/7/96 © 1996 United Feature Syndicate, Inc.(NYC)
WHAT IF IT'S A LIFE-THREATENING PROBLEM?
THAT REMINDS ME, THE CAFETERIA WON'T BE LABELING THE ENTREES ANYMORE.

I'M GOING TO TRY MY PAW AT BEING A CAREER COUNSELOR.
S.Adams

INSECURE PEOPLE WILL SEEK MY ADVICE AND I'LL TELL THEM TO BE MORE SELF-RELIANT.

5/8/96 © 1996 United Feature Syndicate, Inc.(NYC)
THAT SOUNDS LAZY AND UNHELPFUL.
WOULD YOU WANT CAREER ADVICE FROM SOMEBODY WHO HAS TO WORK HARD?

DOGBERT, CAREER COUNSELOR
YOU CAN'T EXPECT YOUR EMPLOYER TO TAKE CARE OF YOU FOREVER, WALLY.

DON'T EXPECT RAISES, DON'T EXPECT TO BE TRAINED AND DON'T EXPECT A PENSION.
S. Adams

THAT'S DEPRESSING. I NEED A SOURBALL.
THOSE ARE MARBLES WRAPPED IN CELLOPHANE.
5/9/96 © 1996 United Feature Syndicate, Inc.(NYC)

DOGBERT, CAREER COUNSELOR
ACCORDING TO YOUR OCCUPATIONAL PREFERENCE TEST, YOU LIKE TO REMOVE VITAL ORGANS FROM HELPLESS PEOPLE.

THAT NARROWS THE CAREER CHOICES TO DOCTOR OR SERIAL KILLER. DO YOU GET ALONG WITH OTHER PEOPLE?
S. Adams

OTHER PEOPLE ARE INSIGNIFICANT INSECTS.
WE'LL HAVE TO GO TO A TIE-BREAKER QUESTION.
5/10/96 © 1996 United Feature Syndicate, Inc.(NYC)

DOGBERT, CAREER COUNSELOR
I'M A LOWLY TECHNICAL WRITER NOW, BUT MY GOAL IS TO BECOME A FAMOUS NOVELIST.

MY PLAN IS TO WRITE WITTY AND SCATHING E-MAIL MESSAGES ABOUT CO-WORKERS UNTIL A PUBLISHER GIVES ME AN ADVANCE.
S. Adams

THEY MIGHT EXPECT YOU TO WRITE A BOOK AT SOME POINT.
BLOOD SUCKERS!
5/11/96 © 1996 United Feature Syndicate, Inc.(NYC)

5/12/96 © 1996 United Feature Syndicate, Inc.

THE COMPANY ANNOUNCED WE'RE BEING BOUGHT BY OUR LONG-TIME RIVAL.
DON'T WORRY ABOUT LAYOFFS. THEY LIKE ENGINEERS. IN FACT, THEY ALREADY HAVE A DIVISION THAT DOES WHAT WE DO!
S. Adams
5/13/96 © 1996 United Feature Syndicate, Inc.(NYC)
EXCEPT THEY'RE YOUNGER AND THEY AREN'T PAID AS MUCH AS WE ARE...
SPIN
AFTER THE MERGER, WE'LL REDUCE STAFF IN AREAS THAT ARE REDUNDANT.
I HOPE THE EMPLOYEES OF THIS COMPANY WILL BE EVALUATED FAIRLY COMPARED TO THOSE IN THE BUYING COMPANY.
S. Adams
5/14/96 © 1996 United Feature Syndicate, Inc.(NYC)
WE ALREADY HAVE A BALD GUY.
DOES YOURS STEAL OFFICE FURNITURE, TOO?
I'M PARALYZED WITH FEAR BECAUSE OF THE PENDING MERGER.
THANKS TO YOUR LEADERSHIP I'VE GONE FROM BEING UNMOTIVATED TO BEING INERT.
S. Adams
5/15/96 © 1996 United Feature Syndicate, Inc.(NYC)
I THINK I'M ADVANCING TO THE NEXT PHASE. HELLO, RIGOR MORTIS!! TAKE ME, I'M READY!!
IT MIGHT BE TIME FOR A MORALE-BOOSTING POTLUCK LUNCH.

IN THE "DUE DILIGENCE" PHASE OF OUR MERGER YOU WILL GIVE US ACCESS TO ALL OF YOUR PROPRIETARY INFORMATION.
S. Adams

WOULDN'T THAT LET YOU KNOW HOW TO CRUSH US COMPETITIVELY? COULDN'T YOU CANCEL THE MERGER AND TAKE OUR CUSTOMERS WITHOUT PAYING A CENT?

MUST... CONTAIN MANIACAL... LAUGH...
5/16/96 © 1996 United Feature Syndicate, Inc. (NYC)

"DUE DILIGENCE" BEFORE THE MERGER.
YOU MUST REVEAL YOUR SECRETS SO MY COMPANY KNOWS WHAT IT'S BUYING.
S. Adams

ALL OF OUR PROJECTS ARE DOOMED. MOST OF THE GOOD EMPLOYEES LEFT. OUR CUSTOMERS ARE STARTING A CLASS ACTION SUIT...

AT LEAST THE BUILDING IS WORTH SOMETHING
IF YOU FEEL A TICKLE, THAT'S ASBESTOS.
5/17/96 © 1996 United Feature Syndicate, Inc. (NYC)

WITH ALL THIS TALK OF "DIVERSITY" THERE'S NO MENTION OF THE PAIN WE SMART CREATURES ENDURE WHILE SURROUNDED BY DOLTS.
S. Adams

GOOD POINT. I DON'T KNOW HOW WE DO IT.

IT LOOKS LIKE I'LL HAVE TO HOLD SECRET MEETINGS.
YEAH, OUR LIVES ARE A CONSTANT STRUGGLE.
5/18/96 © 1996 United Feature Syndicate, Inc. (NYC)

DOGBERT'S DREAM ANALYSIS
I WAS IN A BIG FIELD FULL OF TOFU AND CARBURETORS.
S. Adams
IT MEANS YOU'RE A GULLIBLE MORON.
THAT'S $25 PLEASE.
THEN I WAS RUNNING, RUNNING, RUNNING AGAINST THE WIND
THAT MEANS YOU'RE UGLY.
THEN THE BUTTERFLY TURNED INTO AN OPERA SINGER.
THAT MEANS YOU'RE BALD.
5/19/96 © 1996 United Feature Syndicate, Inc.
SUDDENLY I SAW A NEW ALGORITHM FOR DATA COMPRESSION.
IT MEANS YOU'RE BORING.
THEN I TOLD THE CAR DEALER I WANTED THE ANTI-RUST SEALANT, THE EXTENDED WARRANTY AND THE LEASE OPTION.
WHAT DO YOU THINK IT MEANS?
IT MEANS I'M GOING TO MAKE SOME SERIOUS MONEY TODAY.

IT HAS ALWAYS BEEN MY GOAL TO BECOME SUPREME RULER OF EARTH...
SAdams

BUT LATELY I'VE BEEN WONDERING IF YOU DOLTS ARE WORTHY OF MY LEADERSHIP.

5/20/96 © 1996 United Feature Syndicate, Inc.(NYC)
DO YOU THINK MAYBE YOUR EGO IS OUT OF CONTROL, DOGBERT?
I LIKE IT THAT WAY.

OUR NEW POLICY FORBIDS THE USE OF WEAPONS OR ANY VIOLENCE IN THE WORKPLACE.
SAdams

UMMM... WHAT WAS THE POLICY BEFORE THIS?

5/21/96 © 1996 United Feature Syndicate, Inc.(NYC)
I'M NOT SURE... MAYBE IF YOU HAD A PERMIT AND IT WAS IN SEASON.
THERE GOES ANOTHER COMPANY BENEFIT.

ALICE, THESE UNSIGHTLY STACKS OF PAPERS ARE A VIOLATION OF MY "CLEAN DESK" POLICY.
ALICE
SAdams

5/22/96 © 1996 United Feature Syndicate, Inc.(NYC)
... AND DON'T EVEN GET ME STARTED ABOUT THE ERGONOMICS OF THIS SITUATION.
WALLY

YESTERDAY I WAS LYING IN A SUN SPOT THINKING ABOUT HOW YOU WORK, WORK, WORK BUT YOUR NET WORTH REMAINS CONSTANT.
S. Adams
HA HA HA HA HA HA!!
5/23/96 © 1996 United Feature Syndicate, Inc.
WELL... I GUESS YOU HAD TO BE THERE.

I HAD A CAT ONCE...
SODA
S. Adams
I PETTED THAT THING FOR TWO HOURS BUT I DIDN'T FEEL ANY BETTER.
5/24/96 © 1996 United Feature Syndicate, Inc. (NYC)
PETTING IS FOR THE BENEFIT OF THE CAT, NOT YOUR HAND.
THEY'RE SO SELFISH.

A TWO PERCENT ANNUAL RAISE?!! WOWEE!!
S. Adams
HA HA! YOU TRIED TO DISAPPOINT ME BUT I COMPENSATED BY DRASTICALLY LOWERING MY EXPECTATIONS!
5/25/96 © 1996 United Feature Syndicate, Inc.
YEAH, IT MIGHT BE A GOOD SIGN, BUT I'M THINKING NOT.
WEEEE!!

5/26/96 © 1996 United Feature Syndicate, Inc.

HE SLIPS IN LIKE A PANTHER TO TAKE THE LAST CUP OF COFFEE AND NOT MAKE MORE.
S. Adams

I AM PHIL, THE PRINCE OF INSUFFICIENT LIGHT! I DARN YOU TO HECK!!!
PHIL?

YOU WERE ALWAYS MOM'S GOLDEN BOY.
SOMEBODY BROUGHT POTATO SALAD. GIVE ME YOUR SPOON.
5/27/96 © 1996 United Feature Syndicate, Inc.(NYC)

MOM WANTED ME TO BE A MANAGER LIKE YOU. BUT I CHOSE MY OWN PATH.
S. Adams

I BECAME PHIL, THE RULER OF HECK, THE PUNISHER OF MINOR SINS!
HOW DO YOU MAKE MONEY?

CORPORATE SPONSORSHIP. "PROCTER AND GAMBLE" PAYS ME TO STAY AWAY FROM THEM.
YOU SHOULD SELL A LINE OF HOME-EXERCISE SPOONS.
5/28/96 © 1996 United Feature Syndicate, Inc.

THIS IS PHIL, RULER OF HECK, WITH A SPECIAL OFFER FOR MY PATENTED "EXERSPOON."
S. Adams

YOU CAN DO OVER SEVEN MILLION EXERCISES WITH THE "EXERSPOON." IT EVEN TRIMS PROBLEM AREAS!

AND THANKS TO THE INNOVATIVE SPOON SHAPE, STORAGE IS A BREEZE!
MMM...
5/29/96 © 1996 United Feature Syndicate, Inc.

I NEED THIS INFORMATION TODAY. PLUS A COMPLETE ANALYSIS OF THE ALTERNATIVES.
CRINKLE CRINKLE STUFF
S.Adams
5/30/96 © 1996 United Feature Syndicate, Inc.
THAT WASN'T NICE.
IN TODAY'S LESSON, YOU LEARN THAT YOU'RE MY CO-WORKER, NOT MY BOSS.
WALLY, I NEED YOUR INPUT ON THIS BY THE END OF THE DAY.
PLEASE DROP YOUR REQUEST HERE, IN "WALLY'S PILE OF PERPETUAL IGNORAGE."
S.Adams
5/31/96 © 1996 United Feature Syndicate, Inc.(NYC)
CAN'T I JUST GIVE IT TO YOU?
I DON'T LIKE TO TOUCH THAT STUFF WITH MY HANDS.
WHEN DILBERT COMES BY, TELL HIM TO ADD "WALK THE TALK" TO HIS PRESENTATION.
HE WANTS YOU TO USE A "WALKIE-TALKIE" TO DO THE PRESENTATION.
S.Adams
6/1/96 © 1996 United Feature Syndicate, Inc.(NYC)
UM... DID HE SAY WHY?
HEY, LOOK AT MY PAYCHECK! I JUST REALIZED I DON'T GET PAID THE BIG BUCKS!

MY NEXT VICTIM.
I AM PHIL, THE PRINCE OF INSUFFICIENT LIGHT AND SUPREME RULER OF HECK!!
HI, PHIL.
YOU MUST CHOOSE ONE OF THESE TWO HIDEOUS FATES TO PAY FOR YOUR SINS.
YOU CAN CHOOSE ETERNAL HIGH PAY, BUT ALL OF YOUR WORK WILL BE BURNED IN FRONT OF YOU AT THE END OF EACH DAY...
OR YOU CAN CHOOSE ETERNAL POVERTY, BUT YOUR WORK WILL BE USEFUL AND APPRECIATED.
WOW! THEY'RE BOTH BETTER THAN MY CURRENT JOB!
HEY, WALLY, YOU MIGHT WANT TO GET IN ON THIS!
I WATCH TV WHEN I'M SUPPOSED TO BE TELE-COMMUTING.
I HATE THE NINETIES.
DO ME FIRST!
S Adams © 1996 United Feature Syndicate, Inc.
6/2/96

HALT AND SUBMIT TO THE MIND SCAN OF "BRAINITOR, THE GUARDIAN OF SECURITY."

THE BAG CONTAINS ONE COMPUTER... "PENTIUM" PROCESSOR... ONE GIG HARD DRIVE... HIGHLY FRAGMENTED...
S.Adams

PLEASE WAIT WHILE I OPTIMIZE YOUR HARD DISK...
THIS IS VAGUELY UNSETTLING.
6/3/96 © 1996 United Feature Syndicate, Inc.(NYC)

DO YOU SEE "TIME" AS A SEQUENCE OF DISCRETE EVENTS OR SIMPLY A LINE OF PERCEPTION THROUGH INFINITE POSSIBILITIES?
TECH EE

I SEE "TIME" AS MORE OF A MAGAZINE.
TECH EE
S.Adams

YOU KNOW THESE MOMENTS WE HAVE TOGETHER — WE REALLY MUST HAVE THEM LESS OFTEN.
ASK ME ABOUT "LIFE."
6/4/96 © 1996 United Feature Syndicate, Inc.(NYC)

ALTHOUGH WE ARE NOTHING BUT POND SCUM IN THIS COMPANY...

IT'S NICE TO KNOW WE CAN STILL FIND SOMEONE OF LOWER STATUS TO TORMENT.
S.Adams

YOU CALL THESE BROCHURES? HOW CAN I EVEN CONSIDER BUYING PRODUCTS FROM A "VEN-DUH" SUCH AS YOU?
TELL ME IF THIS HURTS.
6/5/96 © 1996 United Feature Syndicate, Inc.(NYC)

TORMENTING THE VENDOR
YOU MUST DO OUR BIDDING, VENDOR. WE CONTROL YOUR ECONOMIC FUTURE.

OF COURSE, OUR BUYING DECISION WILL BE BASED SOLELY ON QUANTIFIABLE PERFORMANCE MEASUREMENTS.
S. Adams

YOUR COMPETITOR COMPLETED THE "VENDOR CHALLENGE COURSE" IN 37 SECONDS.
AND HE GAVE US VERY NICE T-SHIRTS.
6/6/96 © 1996 United Feature Syndicate, Inc.(NYC)

DILBERT, I FOUND YOUR FATHER. HE'S BEEN AT THE "ALL YOU CAN EAT" RESTAURANT IN THE MALL SINCE 1989.

HE'S SO LITERAL – HE DIDN'T WANT TO LEAVE UNTIL IT WAS "ALL HE COULD EAT."
S. Adams

WHEN'S HE COMING HOME?
I'M THINKING OF JOINING HIM. HE GOT A BOOTH.
6/7/96 © 1996 United Feature Syndicate, Inc.(NYC)

I CAN'T BELIEVE YOUR FATHER HAS BEEN LIVING IN THE "ALL YOU CAN EAT" RESTAURANT SINCE 1989!

YOU HAVE THE ODDEST FAMILY. WHAT DID HE LOOK LIKE WHEN YOU SAW HIM AFTER ALL THESE YEARS?
S. Adams

I HAVEN'T SEEN HIM YET. I'M WAITING FOR "BURRITO NIGHT."
NOW IS WHEN YOU SHOULD BE SAYING "JUST KIDDING."
6/9/96 © 1996 United Feature Syndicate, Inc.(NYC)

WHERE'S DOGBERT?
UH-OH.
ARE YOU GULLIBLE? DO YOU SPEND MONEY ON STUPID STUFF?
CALL THE "DOGBERT GULLIBLE FRIENDS HOTLINE" FOR HELP. ONLY FOUR DOLLARS PER MINUTE.
HELLO, DOGBERT. I BOUGHT AN EXERCISE MACHINE AND I'M STILL LAZY.
PLEASE HOLD.
OKAY!
CALL NOW, AND I'LL REPLACE YOUR OLD TELEVISION WITH A NEW ONE THAT LOOKS JUST LIKE IT, WHILE YOU SLEEP!
IF YOU DON'T HAVE A TOUCH TONE PHONE, STAY ON THE LINE...
UNTIL YOU GET ONE.
S. Adams
6/9/96 © 1996 United Feature Syndicate, Inc.

THESE ARE SOME OF THE ADVANCED MATERIALS I'M DESIGNING AT WORK. THAT JAR HOLDS A PYROPHORIC SUBSTANCE.
LET'S SEE.
S.Adams

FLASH

YEP, THAT'S A GOOD BATCH.
A PERSON FROM A SMARTER GENDER MIGHT HAVE SAID "WHAT DOES 'PYROPHORIC' MEAN?"
6/10/96 © 1996 United Feature Syndicate, Inc.(NYC)

THE DOGBERT CONSULTING COMPANY WILL HELP US DESIGN A NEW COMPANY LOGO.
S.Adams

GLUG GLUG GLUG

WHEN WILL YOU START?
I JUST FINISHED. I CALL IT THE BROWN RING OF QUALITY.
6/11/96 © 1996 United Feature Syndicate, Inc.(NYC)

YOUR NEW LOGO MIGHT LOOK LIKE A SIMPLE COFFEE STAIN, BUT WHAT DOES THE IMAGE SAY ABOUT YOU?
S.Adams

WE'RE SLOPPY AND UNIMAGI-NATIVE?
WE GIVE LOTS OF MONEY TO CONSULTANTS AND GET LITTLE IN RETURN?

WOW. THIS IS ALMOST TOO GOOD.
OOH OOH! HOW ABOUT "OUR OPINIONS DON'T MATTER"?
6/12/96 © 1996 United Feature Syndicate, Inc.(NYC)

OUR OBJECTIVES ARE UNCLEAR AND OUR MISSION STATEMENT IS GIBBERISH...
BUT THANKS TO AN ARTIFICIAL SENSE OF URGENCY, I'M WORKING HARDER THAN EVER!
WHAT'S THE GOOD NEWS YOU SAID YOU HAVE?
APPARENTLY I'M INSANE. BUT I'M ONE OF THE HAPPY KINDS!
S.Adams
6/13/96 © 1996 United Feature Syndicate, Inc.(NYC)

THIS COMPANY MAKES PERFECT SENSE, NOW THAT I'M INSANE.
FOR EXAMPLE, IT MIGHT SEEM AS THOUGH WE'RE WOEFULLY UNDERSTAFFED, BUT I CAN COMPENSATE BY WORKING SMARTER NOT HARDER.
HEY, IF I'M CAPABLE OF WORKING SMARTER, THEN WHY DO I WORK HERE?
THE HEALING HAS BEGUN.
S.Adams
6/14/96 © 1996 United Feature Syndicate, Inc.(NYC)

DILBERT, I NOTICE YOU'VE BEEN LOOKING DEPRESSED LATELY.
HERE'S A PRESCRIPTION FOR AN ANTIDEPRESSANT DRUG. BE SURE TO EXERCISE REGULARLY AND DON'T SKIP MEALS.
WHAT MAKES YOU THINK YOU'RE QUALIFIED TO DIAGNOSE MY MENTAL HEALTH?!!
I'D BETTER DOUBLE IT.
S.Adams
6/15/96 © 1996 United Feature Syndicate, Inc.(NYC)

6/6/96 © 1996 United Feature Syndicate, Inc.

S. Adams

THE STATUS OF MY ACTION ITEM IS 50% DONE.

SPECIFICALLY, I FINISHED THE ITEM PART BUT NOT THE ACTION.
S.Adams

DO YOU HAVE AN ESTIMATE FOR WHEN THE ACTION WILL BE DONE?
YES, AND THAT ESTIMATE IS 100% COMPLETE!
6/17/96 © 1996 United Feature Syndicate, Inc.

10
INJURY FREE DAYS
S.Adams

BAM!
AAAEEIII!!
R-R-ROLL
THUD

THIS IS VERY IRONIC.
NO, IT WAS IRONIC WHEN IT HAPPENED ELEVEN DAYS AGO.
6/19/96 © 1996 United Feature Syndicate, Inc.(NYC)

SOME IDIOT STOOD ON A CHAIR AND FELL OFF.

NOW WE ALL HAVE TO TAKE TWELVE HOURS OF CHAIR SAFETY TRAINING.
S.Adams

IS THAT A "DO" OR A "NOT DO"?
6/19/96 © 1996 United Feature Syndicate, Inc.(NYC)

CAROL, I ASKED YOU TO ENROLL ME IN THE QUALITY COLLEGE, BUT THE CONFIRMATION SAYS CLOWN COLLEGE.

IT'S A PREREQUISITE COURSE.
S. Adams

THIS IS GONNA COST ME ON SECRETARIES DAY.
I HOPE IT'S OKAY TO BE AN ANGRY CLOWN.
6/20/96 © 1996 United Feature Syndicate, Inc.

I WAS GOING TO GET THE "BUNS OF STEEL" VIDEO BUT I'M MAKING EXCELLENT PROGRESS WITHOUT IT.

WHEN THEY SAY STEEL, IT REFERS TO HARDNESS, NOT WEIGHT.
S. Adams

I KNEW IT SEEMED TOO EASY.
STAY AWAY FROM LARGE MAGNETS.
6/21/96 © 1996 United Feature Syndicate, Inc.(NYC)

THE ONLY EMPLOYEE SUGGESTIONS THAT GET ACCEPTED ARE THE ONES THAT ARE HARMLESS AND STUPID.

I SUBMITTED SOME HARMLESS AND STUPID IDEAS TO TEST MY THEORY.
S. Adams

SUGGESTION: REPLACE ALL #2 PENCILS WITH #4 PENCILS. THE HARD LEAD LASTS LONGER YET COSTS THE SAME.
THAT COULD WORK.
6/22/96 © 1996 United Feature Syndicate, Inc.(NYC)

I WON'T ALWAYS BE AROUND TO BE YOUR MENTOR, ASOK.
SO I'VE CAPTURED ALL OF MY CAREER WISDOM IN THIS SOFTWARE, WHICH I CALL THE "AUTOMENTOR."
S. Adams
AUTOMENTOR, HOW CAN I ACHIEVE JOB SATISFACTION?
TRY GIVING YOURSELF A MASSAGE IN YOUR CUBICLE.
AUTOMENTOR, HOW CAN I MAKE SURE MY ACCOMPLISHMENTS GET NOTICED?
THAT'S NOT A PROBLEM AT THIS COMPANY; NOBODY ACCOMPLISHES ANYTHING.
6/23/96 © 1996 United Feature Syndicate, Inc.
SHOULD I LOOK FOR A NEW JOB?
TOO LATE. THEY DON'T CALL THIS PLACE THE "RÉSUMÉ STAIN" FOR NOTHING.
HOW DO YOU HANDLE ALL THE HOPELESSNESS?
I GIVE IT TO THE NEW GUY.

HERE'S A DRAFT OF MY NEW OBJECTIVES. I TRIED TO MAKE THEM ACHIEVABLE.
"NO MATTER HOW STUPID MY CO-WORKERS ARE, I WILL NOT PUNCH A HOLE IN ANYONE'S TORSO, RIP OUT A VITAL ORGAN AND KEEP IT IN MY CUBICLE AS A WARNING TO OTHERS."
S.Adams
I HOPE SHE GETS THOSE OBJECTIVES APPROVED.
YES! IT'S MEASURABLE!
6/24/96 © 1996 United Feature Syndicate, Inc.(NYC)

I COULD SIT HERE DOING NOTHING.
OR I COULD IMPLEMENT A BOLD QUALITY INITIATIVE WITH THE HELP OF MY TALENTED AND ENERGETIC COWORKERS.
S.Adams
I CRACK ME UP.
6/25/96 © 1996 United Feature Syndicate, Inc.(NYC)

WHAT EXACTLY IS THE DOGBERT DAY CARE CONCEPT ?
PROGRESSIVE COMPANIES CAN PROVIDE DAY CARE WITHOUT SPENDING A BUNDLE.
S.Adams
WOULDN'T WE SPEND A FORTUNE ON DUCT TAPE?
IT'S REUSABLE UNLESS IT GETS SLOBBERED ON.
6/26/96 © 1996 United Feature Syndicate, Inc.

ALICE, I NEED TO GATHER SOME REQUIREMENTS BEFORE DESIGNING THE COMPANY CHILD CARE FACILITY.
DO YOU MIND IF YOUR CHILDREN SPEND THE DAY SEWING GARMENTS IN A WINDOWLESS ROOM FULL OF ILLEGAL ALIENS?
I MIND.
S. Adams
I'LL PUT YOU DOWN AS A MAYBE.
WOULD I GET DISCOUNTS ON THOSE GARMENTS?
6/27/96 © 1996 United Feature Syndicate, Inc. (NYC)

HERE'S MY FINAL PLAN FOR THE COMPANY'S DAY CARE FACILITY.
I CALL IT FREE RANGE DAY CARE. THE CHILDREN ARE ALLOWED TO ROAM FREE AMONG THE CUBICLES. IT'S VERY ECONOMICAL.
S. Adams
I DON'T BELIEVE HE'S REALLY AN EVIL TROLL.
LOOK AT THE "POWERPOINT" SLIDES HE'S MAKING. IT'S NOT HUMAN.
6/28/96 © 1996 United Feature Syndicate, Inc.

THE RESULTS OF THE EMPLOYEE SATISFACTION SURVEY ARE IN. SCORES FOR MY DEPARTMENT ARE DISMAL.
I'M ASSIGNING YOU TO THE SATISFACTION TASK FORCE UNTIL THE PROBLEM IS SOLVED.
S. Adams
PLEASE... ANYTHING BUT THAT...
HOW SATISFIED ARE YOU NOW?
6/29/96 © 1996 United Feature Syndicate, Inc.

I CALL MY INVENTION THE D-CHIP TELEVISION FILTER.
I FEEL SAFER ALREADY.
IT SCREENS OUT ANY SHOW WITH VIOLENCE.
S. Adams
THERE GOES THE NEWS, SPORTS AND DRAMAS.
IT ALSO GETS RID OF SHOWS THAT FEATURE DISHONESTY OR SEXUAL INNUENDOS.
GOODBYE COMEDY AND COMMERCIALS.
LET'S HOOK IT UP.
6/30/96 © 1996 United Feature Syndicate, Inc.
ALL WE'RE GETTING IS WEATHER REPORTS.
A HUGE TORNADO RIPPED THROUGH A BEEP SSSS SSSSSSSSS
IT WORKS! THE EVIL CAN'T GET TO US NOW, DOGBERT.
UNHOOK THAT #!*% THING OR I'LL RIP OFF YOUR LEG AND BEAT YOU TO DEATH WITH IT.

RATBERT, MY COMPANY IS HIRING FOR OUR QUALITY ASSURANCE GROUP. YOU'D BE PERFECT.
WHAT WOULD I HAVE TO DO?
YOU WOULD FIND FLAWS IN OUR NEW PRODUCT, THUS MAKING YOURSELF AN OBJECT OF INTENSE HATRED AND RIDICULE.
S. Adams
BUT THEN YOU'D FIX THOSE FLAWS... AND YOUR RESPECT FOR ME WOULD GROW INTO A SPECIAL BOND OF FRIENDSHIP, RIGHT?!
NO, THEN WE SHIP.
7/1/96 © 1996 United Feature Syndicate, Inc.(NYC)

I'D BE PERFECT FOR THE JOB IN QUALITY ASSURANCE. HERE'S MY RESUME.
ARE YOU BOTHERED BY THE FACT THAT HALF OF YOUR WORDS ARE SPELLED WRONG?
NOPE! I'M NOT EVEN BOTHERED BY YOUR ANAL-RETENTIVE BEHAVIOR.
S. Adams
YOU'RE HIRED. YOUR BONUS WILL EQUAL NEGATIVE 100% OF YOUR BASE SALARY. OKAY?
I DON'T SEE ANY PROBLEM WITH THAT.
7/2/96 © 1996 United Feature Syndicate, Inc.(NYC)

MY QUALITY ASSURANCE REVIEW OF YOUR BETA PRODUCT TURNED UP A FEW BUGS, WALLY.
I'VE CLASSIFIED THE BUGS BY SEVERITY: 1) LETHAL, 2) BONEHEADED, 3) VEXING.
S. Adams
ALL I SEE ARE LETHAL AND VEXING. WHERE'S BONEHEADED?
I'M TRYING TO RENT A STADIUM TO HOLD THE PRINTOUT.
7/3/96 © 1996 United Feature Syndicate, Inc.(NYC)

IN THE SHORT TIME YOU'VE WORKED IN QUALITY ASSURANCE, YOU'VE FOUND A HUGE NUMBER OF FLAWS IN OUR PROTOTYPE.
THAT'S MY JOB!
S. Adams

YOU'RE JEOPARDIZING OUR SCHEDULE. THE ENTIRE PROJECT WILL FAIL AND IT'S ALL YOUR FAULT.
WHY IS IT MY FAULT?

IF A TREE FALLS IN THE FOREST... AND WE'VE ALREADY SOLD THE TREE... DOES IT HAVE QUALITY?
HOW MANY ANGELS CAN DANCE ON YOUR HEAD?
7/4/96 © 1996 United Feature Syndicate, Inc.(NYC)

LET'S HAVE A LITTLE PREMEETING TO PREPARE FOR THE MEETING TOMORROW.

WHOA! DO YOU THINK IT'S SAFE TO JUMP RIGHT INTO THE PREMEETING WITHOUT PLANNING IT?
S. Adams

OKAY, LET'S GET THIS PRELIMINARY PREMEETING MEETING GOING.
YOU THINK YOU'RE FUNNY, BUT YOU'RE NOT.
7/5/96 © 1996 United Feature Syndicate, Inc.(NYC)

I COULDN'T HELP NOTICING THE BUGS IN THE PROGRAM ON THIS OLD DISKETTE YOU THREW AWAY.

I FIXED THE BUGS AND TIGHTENED THE CODE FROM TWELVE THOUSAND LINES TO SIXTEEN.
S. Adams

IT TOOK ME THREE MONTHS TO WRITE THAT PROGRAM.
I TOOK THE LIBERTY OF UPDATING YOUR RESUME. I'M GUESSING YOU'LL NEED IT SOON.
7/6/96 © 1996 United Feature Syndicate, Inc.(NYC)

I'LL BE WRITING YOUR PERFORMANCE REVIEW THIS AFTERNOON.
BUT THIS MORNING I'M HELPING MY DAUGHTER SELL CUB GIRL COOKIES.
S. Adams
FOR YOUR SHOPPING CONVENIENCE I HAVE ASSIGNED A NAME TO EACH VOLUME LEVEL.
ZERO TO FOUR BOXES IS THE "DOWNSIZER" VOLUME...
FIVE TO EIGHT BOXES IS THE "LOW PERFORMER" VOLUME LEVEL.
7/7/96 © 1996 United Feature Syndicate, Inc.
LET'S SAY SIX HUNDRED BOXES.
AHH... THE "FAST TRACKER." AN EXCELLENT CHOICE.
WHAT'S YOUR DAUGHTER'S NAME?
OOH... GOTTA GO.
I ONLY BOUGHT TWELVE BOXES. NOW I'M THE "UNITED WAY" CHAIRPERSON.
I JUST SIGNED YOUR NAME FOR SIX HUNDRED MORE.

SOMEDAY WHEN I BECOME THE SUPREME RULER OF EARTH...
S. Adams
I'LL ORDER EVERYBODY TO GO OUTSIDE ONCE A DAY AND RUN AROUND WITH THEIR MOUTHS OPEN.
7/8/96 © 1996 United Feature Syndicate, Inc.(NYC)
BECAUSE YOU SUPPORT FRESH AIR AND EXERCISE?
BECAUSE I HATE FLIES.
THANKS FOR MAKING THAT PRODUCT MOCK-UP LAST WEEK. THE CUSTOMER LIKED IT SO MUCH THAT HE ORDERED A THOUSAND!
S. Adams
THAT WAS A MOCK-UP! WE DON'T MAKE THAT PRODUCT YET. IT WOULD TAKE THREE YEARS TO MAKE ONE.
7/9/96 © 1996 United Feature Syndicate, Inc.(NYC)
JUST GIVE ME A THOUSAND MOCK-UPS. THE FIRST ONE WAS TERRIFIC!
THE MOCK-UP WAS OUR COMPETITOR'S PRODUCT WITH DUCT TAPE OVER THE LOGO.
I'LL NEED YOUR FULL MANAGEMENT SUPPORT IN THIS MEETING WITH SALES.
JUST WATCH THE MASTER AT WORK.
S. Adams
I PROMISED A CUSTOMER A PRODUCT THAT WE DON'T MAKE. YOU NEED TO ENGINEER-UP A THOUSAND UNITS BY EARLY NEXT WEEK.
IS THURSDAY OKAY?
7/10/96 © 1996 United Feature Syndicate, Inc.(NYC)
WAIT UNTIL HE FINDS OUT THAT THURSDAY ISN'T "EARLY NEXT WEEK." HEE HEE!

I'M ASSIGNING EACH OF YOU TO A SEPARATE "QUALITY" INITIATIVE.
S.Adams

IS THERE ANY RISK THIS WILL DEVOUR OUR PRODUCTIVE HOURS, LOWER OUR MORALE AND HAVE NO IMPACT ON OUR PROFITABILITY?

AND WE'LL HAVE A CONTEST TO COME UP WITH A NAME FOR THE OVERALL INITIATIVE.
HOW ABOUT "QUALICIDE"?
7/11/96 © 1996 United Feature Syndicate, Inc.(NYC)

HE'S WITH THE OTHER MANAGERS IN AN EMPLOYEE RANKING AND RATING SESSION.
S.Adams

YOUR SALARY DEPENDS ON HOW WELL YOUR BOSS CAN DEFEND YOUR PROPOSED RAISE TO THE OTHER MANAGERS.
SOB

I'M FAIRLY SURE THIS DILBERT GUY WORKS FOR YOU.
DOESN'T RING A BELL.
7/12/96 © 1996 United Feature Syndicate, Inc.(NYC)

CATBERT, THE EVIL DIRECTOR OF HUMAN RESOURCES
WALLY, IT'S TIME FOR YOUR MANDATORY BLOOD TEST.

I DON'T TAKE DRUGS.
I'M TESTING TO SEE IF YOU'RE STEALING TIME FROM THE COMPANY.
S.Adams

TIME? HOW CAN YOU TEST FOR THAT?
WE TEST YOUR GENERAL HEALTH. IF IT'S GOOD, YOU'RE NOT WORKING ENOUGH HOURS.
YOU THIEF.
7/13/96 © 1996 United Feature Syndicate, Inc.(NYC)

ACCORDING TO THIS PHONE BILL, YOU'VE BEEN MAKING PERSONAL CALLS.
THAT'S LIKE STEALING FROM THE COMPANY, ALICE.
S. Adams
MUST... CONTROL... FIST... OF... DEATH...
I SPENT EIGHTY CENTS TO TELL MY FAMILY I WAS WORKING LATE.
HERE'S A DOLLAR. THE EXTRA TWENTY CENTS IS FOR THE PERSONAL THOUGHT THAT I'M ABOUT TO HAVE ON COMPANY TIME.
7/4/96 © 1996 United Feature Syndicate, Inc.
MMM
AND HERE'S MY BILL FOR $40,000 IN UNPAID OVERTIME THAT THE COMPANY STOLE FROM ME.
THAT'S NOT STEALING; THAT'S BEING COMPETITIVE.
I THINK I'LL BE COMPETITIVE WITH A FEW BUSHELS OF OFFICE SUPPLIES LATER TODAY.

CATBERT, THE EVIL DIRECTOR OF HUMAN RESOURCES
ACCORDING TO MY SOURCES, YOU'VE BEEN ENJOYING YOUR JOB, WALLY.
S.Adams
IT WAS TEMPORARY. I DON'T KNOW WHAT GOT INTO ME...
PLEASE REFER TO PAGE ONE OF THE EMPLOYEE MANUAL.
7/15/96 © 1996 United Feature Syndicate, Inc.(NYC)
"JOB SATISFACTION IS THE SAME AS STEALING FROM THE COMPANY."
I'LL HAVE TO CHARGE YOU FOR ADMISSION UNLESS I START HEARING SOME SHRIEKS OF PAIN.

IN THE YEAR THAT WE'VE DATED, LIZ, YOU'VE OFTEN MENTIONED VARIOUS PROBLEMS IN YOUR LIFE.
S.Adams
I HAVE COMPILED THOSE PROBLEMS INTO A LIST OF REQUIREMENTS AND DEVELOPED A COMPREHENSIVE SET OF SOLUTIONS.
7/16/96 © 1996 United Feature Syndicate, Inc.(NYC)
HOW THOUGHTFUL. I DIDN'T EVEN KNOW I WAS BROKEN.
NO, NO, NOT BROKEN... JUST A BIT BUGGY.

UM... WHEN I'VE SHARED MY FEELINGS WITH YOU, I WASN'T HOPING YOU'D DESIGN AN ACTION PLAN TO SOLVE ALL OF MY PROBLEMS.
S.Adams
WHY ELSE WOULD YOU TELL ME ALL OF YOUR PROBLEMS... UNLESS IT'S SOME DEMENTED PLOT TO MAKE YOURSELF FEEL BETTER AT MY EXPENSE?
7/17/96 © 1996 United Feature Syndicate, Inc.(NYC)
YOU WERE RIGHT. IT WAS ALL A DEMENTED PLOT.
I'M TRYING TO GRADUALLY LIFT YOUR VEIL OF IGNORANCE.

OUR NEW "RECOGNITION PROGRAM" ASSIGNS THE NAMES OF PRECIOUS GEMS TO YOUR LEVELS OF PERFORMANCE.
S. Adams
THE HIGHEST LEVEL IS DIAMOND. YOU GET A NEW RING AT EACH LEVEL.
7/19/96 © 1996 United Feature Syndicate, Inc.(NYC)
ARE YOU SURE TALC IS A PRECIOUS GEM?
I THINK I SAW IT SPARKLE.
AS YOU CAN SEE FROM MY RING, I'M A MEMBER OF THE "TALC CLUB" AT WORK.
S. Adams
WITH HARD WORK AND A BIT OF LUCK I WILL RISE TO THE NEXT LEVEL: SHALE.
7/19/96 © 1996 United Feature Syndicate, Inc.(NYC)
I CAN HONESTLY SAY MY RESPECT FOR YOU HAS NEVER BEEN HIGHER.
SOMEDAY, GOD WILLING, I'LL MAKE IT TO ALUMINUM.
IT'S TIME FOR ME TO UPDATE YOUR OBJECTIVES, ALICE.
S. Adams
WE NEED TARGETS THAT CAN ONLY BE ACHIEVED BY AMAZINGLY HARD WORK PLUS THE CONSTANT SUPPORT OF MANAGEMENT.
7/20/96 © 1996 United Feature Syndicate, Inc.(NYC)
I'M BUSY, SO YOU'LL HAVE TO WRITE THEM YOURSELF.
WHAT'S WRONG WITH THIS PICTURE?

DOGBERT, DO YOU THINK LOVE IS THE STRONGEST FORCE IN THE UNIVERSE?
NO, I'D HAVE TO GO WITH STUPIDITY.
S. Adams
FOLLOWED CLOSELY BY ITS COUSIN IGNORANCE.
MORNING BREATH IS NUMBER THREE. THANKS FOR REMINDING ME.
THEN YOU'VE GOT SELFISHNESS, LUST, FEAR, MONEY AND LUCK.
7/21/96 © 1996 United Feature Syndicate, Inc.
BUT LOVE IS IN THE TOP TEN, RIGHT?
IT'S FOURTEENTH, RIGHT AFTER FOOLISH OPTIMISM.
SOMEONE NEEDS HIS LITTLE ROUND BACK SCRATCHED.
DO NOT.
WHERE'S LOVE NOW?
IT'S DOWN AND TO THE LEFT...
LEFT!! LEFT!! LEFT!!
OOWAHH...

NOW THAT JOB SECURITY IS A THING OF THE PAST, I'VE NOTICED THAT MY COMPANY LOYALTY HAS VANISHED, TOO.
S. Adams
AND WHEN YOU MADE MY BONUS PRIMARILY DEPENDENT ON THE BLUNDERS OF SENIOR MANAGEMENT, MY MOTIVATION FLUTTERED AWAY LIKE A LONELY SPARROW.
7/22/96 © 1996 United Feature Syndicate, Inc.(NYC)
SO YOUR POINT IS?
NO POINT. I JUST DIDN'T HAVE ANY REASON TO BE WORKING.
I MAY BE AN IGNORANT RAT, BUT THAT'S OKAY BECAUSE IGNORANCE IS... UM... UM...
S. Adams
BLISS... IGNORANCE IS BLISS.
7/23/96 © 1996 United Feature Syndicate, Inc.(NYC)
OH, GREAT. NOW IT'S GONE.
OOPS
I ADMIT I WAS SKEPTICAL WHEN YOU SAID I WOULD BE EMPOWERED TO MAKE MY OWN DECISIONS...
S. Adams
BUT I GIVE YOU CREDIT. YOU'VE LET ME WORK INDEPENDENTLY FOR THREE MONTHS...
WHAT'S THAT LOOK ON YOUR FACE?
7/24/96 © 1996 United Feature Syndicate, Inc.
PLEASE TELL ME THAT IT WAS EMPOWERMENT I WAS EXPERIENCING.
DID I EVER MENTION THAT YOUR PROJECT WAS CANCELED?

IT LOOKS LIKE WE'LL RELEASE OUR NEW PRODUCT ON TIME, DESPITE ITS MANY DEFECTS.

WE'VE MINIMIZED THE ECONOMIC IMPACT OF THE DEFECTS VIA AN ADVANCED BUSINESS PROCESS CALLED "HOPING NOBODY NOTICES."
S.Adams

AND WE'VE DOUBLED OUR PROJECTED INCOME BY MODIFYING OUR ASSUMPTIONS!
A LOT OF THIS JOB IS MENTAL.
7/25/96 © 1996 United Feature Syndicate, Inc.(NYC)

HERE IN THE "DOGBERT INSTITUTE FOR ADVANCED THINKING," I HAVE DEVISED A PLAN FOR ENDING POVERTY.

MY PLAN IS TO WAIT UNTIL THERE ARE SO MANY TALK SHOWS ON TELEVISION THAT ALL THE PEOPLE WITH WRETCHED LIVES CAN BE PAID GUESTS.
S.Adams

WHAT ABOUT THE POOR PEOPLE WHO DON'T WANT TO BE ON TALK SHOWS?
WE'LL GET THE STRAGGLERS ON "COPS."
7/26/96 © 1996 United Feature Syndicate, Inc.(NYC)

FROM NOW ON, I WILL NOT TRY TO REASON WITH THE IDIOTS I ENCOUNTER. I WILL DISMISS THEM BY WAVING MY PAW AND SAYING "BAH."

JUST BECAUSE SOMEONE THINKS DIFFERENTLY FROM YOU DOESN'T MEAN HE'S AN IDIOT, DOGBERT.
S.Adams

BAH.
7/27/96 © 1996 United Feature Syndicate, Inc.(NYC)

THE BUDGET TRAP
I NEED A QUICK ESTIMATE FOR HOW MUCH YOUR NEXT PROJECT WILL COST, WALLY.
HOW SHOULD I KNOW? YOU HAVEN'T EVEN TOLD ME WHAT MY NEXT PROJECT IS.
THAT'S OKAY. I ONLY NEED A ROUGH ESTIMATE FOR PLANNING PURPOSES.
I SEE WHERE THIS IS GOING. YOU'RE GOING TO TURN MY WILD GUESS INTO A BUDGET. LATER I'LL BE BLAMED WHEN IT'S WRONG.
NO, NO. I WON'T HOLD YOU TO THESE NUMBERS.
WELL...OKAY, LET'S SAY TWO MILLION DOLLARS.
OOH...CAN'T AFFORD THAT. I'LL PUT YOU DOWN FOR TWENTY THOUSAND DOLLARS.
ONE YEAR LATER...
YOU'RE WAY OVER BUDGET. CAN YOU SHOW ME THE CAUSE?
IT DEPENDS. CAN MIRRORS REFLECT YOUR IMAGE?
S Adams
7/28/96 © 1996 United Feature Syndicate, Inc.

LARRY, I'M HERE TO ANNOUNCE MY CANDIDACY FOR SUPREME RULER OF THE UNIVERSE.

THAT'S FUNNY! TELL US ABOUT YOUR NEXT MOVIE, SHARON.
I'M NOT SHARON STONE. I SAID THAT TO GET ON THE SHOW.
S. Adams

SO... WHEN I EMBRACED YOU BEFORE THE SHOW...
I THINK WE'RE BOTH GLAD I HAVE NO VISIBLE MOUTH.
7/29/96 © 1996 United Feature Syndicate, Inc.(NYC)

VOTE FOR ME AND I WILL REFORM THE TAX CODE SO THAT ONLY IDIOTS HAVE TO PAY TAXES!

YAHOO!!
DOGBERT
DOGBERT
DOGBERT
S. Adams

I HOPE NOBODY ASKS ME TO DEFINE "IDIOTS."
...SO, UNDER YOUR PLAN I WOULDN'T PAY ANY TAXES, RIGHT?
7/30/96 © 1996 United Feature Syndicate, Inc.

I'M FROM THE ASSOCIATION FOR PRODUCTS THAT ARE BAD FOR YOU. HERE'S A GENEROUS CONTRIBUTION TO YOUR CAMPAIGN.

THIS IS SO COOL! I'LL USE YOUR MONEY TO GET ELECTED, THEN I'LL PUT YOUR ENTIRE INDUSTRY IN PRISON TO COVER MY TRACKS!
S. Adams

THIS PROBABLY WRECKS MY CHANCES OF BEING NAMED BRIBER OF THE MONTH.
7/31/96 © 1996 United Feature Syndicate, Inc.(NYC)

8/1/96 © 1996 United Feature Syndicate, Inc.(NYC)

8/2/96 © 1996 United Feature Syndicate, Inc.(NYC)

8/3/96 © 1996 United Feature Syndicate, Inc.(NYC)

S. Adams
8/4/96 © 1996 United Feature Syndicate, Inc.

TOM, YOU DELICIOUS HUNK OF BURNING LOVE: IF YOU WERE IN MY CUBICLE NOW I'D...
S.Adams

IT LOOKS AS IF I'M WORKING. NOBODY CAN TELL THAT I'M SENDING STEAMY E-MAIL TO MY NEW BOYFRIEND.

8/5/96 © 1996 United Feature Syndicate, Inc.(NYC)
TINA, TWO THINGS: WATCH OUT FOR THE "SEND TO ALL" ADDRESS, AND THANK YOU VERY MUCH.

I ACCIDENTALLY SENT MY TORRID LOVE LETTER TO EVERY PERSON ON OUR E-MAIL SYSTEM.

SHOULD I HIDE FOREVER OR CAN I COUNT ON THE PROFESSIONALISM OF MY CO-WORKERS?
S.Adams

8/6/96 © 1996 United Feature Syndicate, Inc.(NYC)
WE'LL COMPLETE OUR "CAREER DAY" TOUR WITH AN EXHIBIT THAT I CALL "TINA, THE RED-FACED MONKEY OF LOVE."
IT'S HIDING.

CATBERT: EVIL HR DIRECTOR
IT HAS COME TO MY ATTENTION THAT YOU USED COMPANY RESOURCES TO SEND E-MAIL TO YOUR BOYFRIEND

I'M WILLING TO OVER-LOOK THIS UGLY INCIDENT IN EXCHANGE FOR FIVE MINUTES OF QUALITY PETTING ON MY SOFT, FURRY BELLY.
S.Adams

8/7/96 © 1996 United Feature Syndicate, Inc.(NYC)
THIS SEEMS SO WRONG.
TRY USING BOTH HANDS.

IT'S TIME TO DO PEER-PERFORMANCE REVIEWS!

REMEMBER, THERE'S A LIMITED BUDGET FOR RAISES. YOUR BEST STRATEGY IS TO SLANDER YOUR CO-WORKERS SO THERE'S MORE MONEY FOR YOU!
S.Adams

I PLAN TO SAY VERY NICE THINGS ABOUT YOU.
NICE TRY, WEASEL-BOY.
MANAGING IS EASY WHEN YOU HATE THE EMPLOYEES.
8/9/96 © 1996 United Feature Syndicate, Inc.(NYC)

WALLY, THESE PEER REVIEWS ARE LIKE THE FAMOUS "PRISONER'S DILEMMA."

IF YOU RAT ON ME BUT I SAY GOOD THINGS ABOUT YOU, YOU GET THE BIGGEST RAISE. BUT IF WE PRAISE EACH OTHER WE CAN BOTH GET A SMALL RAISE.
S.Adams

WALLY, IF YOU RAT HIM OUT, I'LL LET YOU LOOK AT MY "VICTORIA'S SECRET" CATALOG.
THIS IS EXACTLY WHY THERE ARE NO COED PRISONS.
8/9/96 © 1996 United Feature Syndicate, Inc.(NYC)

YOU EMPLOYEES ARE THE KEY TO OUR ECONOMIC SUCCESS.

ANYTIME WE NEED A LITTLE STOCK-PRICE BOOST, WE JUST FIRE ANOTHER BATCH OF YOU. IT'S LIKE PRINTING MONEY!
S.Adams

IN FACT, "INCOMPETENCE" HAS BECOME OUR MOST PROFITABLE PRODUCT.
WOW. IT BEAT OUT "LYING TO CUSTOMERS."
8/10/96 © 1996 United Feature Syndicate, Inc.(NYC)

THIS VOICE-MAIL MESSAGE IS FOR THE WHOLE DEPARTMENT.
EVERY MORNING FROM NOW ON YOU'LL GET MY "QUALITY THOUGHT OF THE DAY."
S. Adams
TODAY'S THOUGHT IS... UM...
© 1996 United Feature Syndicate, Inc.
LET'S SEE... ACCORDING TO WEBSTER'S DICTIONARY...
AARDVARK IS A BURROWING AFRICAN MAMMAL THAT EATS ANTS.
WHAT IF WE WERE MORE LIKE THAT?
8/11/96
I MEAN LIKE THE AARDVARK, NOT THE ANTS...
THAT'S WEIRD. EVERY TIME I LEAVE MY QUALITY THOUGHT OF THE DAY, THE SHARED PRINTER STARTS SPEWING RÉSUMÉS.

CATBERT: EVIL HR DIRECTOR
HEY, WALLY... BIG LAYOFFS COMING.
S.Adams

I'VE SEEN THE LIST. I KNOW MORE ABOUT YOUR FUTURE THAN YOU DO. BUT IT'S A SECRET.

SADLY, CATS DON'T KEEP SECRETS VERY WELL.
NICE CHAIR.
8/12/96 © 1996 United Feature Syndicate, Inc.(NYC)

WE DON'T DO "LAYOFFS" AT THIS COMPANY. BUT YOU HAVE BEEN SELECTED TO PARTICIPATE IN OUR MOBILITY POOL!
S.Adams

AS THE NAME IMPLIES, YOU GET TO SCURRY AROUND TRYING TO FIND A NONEXISTENT INTERNAL JOB BEFORE THE AX FALLS.

HOW'S THIS DIFFERENT FROM A LAYOFF?
WITH LAYOFFS YOU GET TO KEEP YOUR DIGNITY.
8/13/96 © 1996 United Feature Syndicate, Inc.(NYC)

I HEAR YOU'RE ON THE LAYOFF LIST, WALLY. HAS ANYONE CLAIMED YOUR CHAIR, YET?
S.Adams

I CLAIMED IT A FEW MINUTES AGO.
LIAR!

I GUESS IT'S TRUE WHAT THEY SAY ABOUT LAYOFFS BEING HARD ON THE SURVIVORS.
OW!
POW!!
8/14/96 © 1996 United Feature Syndicate, Inc.

DOGBERT: CAREER COUNSELOR
I WAS FIRED ONCE, BUT I CAME BACK AS A CONTRACT EMPLOYEE. LATER I WAS REHIRED AT A HIGHER SALARY.
S.Adams

NOW I'M BEING DOWN-SIZED AGAIN. DO YOU THINK THEY'LL BE DUMB ENOUGH TO HIRE ME A THIRD TIME?

YOUR STORY REMINDS ME OF THE PARABLE OF THE ANT AND THE SPIDER.
REALLY? HOW?
THEY'RE BOTH BORING.
8/15/96 © 1996 United Feature Syndicate, Inc.(NYC)

DOGBERT: CAREER COUNSELOR
THE COMPANY WON'T LAY YOU OFF IF ENOUGH PEOPLE QUIT FIRST.
S.Adams

YOUR BEST STRATEGY IS TO CONVINCE YOUR CO-WORKERS THAT THEIR JOBS ARE INTOLERABLE.

WE DO THIS FOR ALL THE YOUNG EMPLOYEES, ASOK. I'LL CAPTURE ON VIDEO THE EXACT MOMENT THAT YOUR LIFE FORCE LEAVES YOUR BODY.
8/16/96 © 1996 United Feature Syndicate, Inc.(NYC)

GOOD NEWS, WALLY. MOST OF OUR SMART EMPLOYEES QUIT TO GET MUCH BETTER JOBS ELSEWHERE. NOW WE DON'T HAVE TO DO ANY DOWNSIZING.
S.Adams

YOUR JOB IS SAFE. WE NEED YOU TO DO THE WORK OF ALL THE PEOPLE WHO LEFT.

IS IT JUST ME... OR IS THE QUALITY OF "GOOD NEWS" REALLY GOING DOWNHILL LATELY?
I'D HAVE TO SAY YOU'RE BOTH GOING DOWNHILL.
8/17/96 © 1996 United Feature Syndicate, Inc.

PEOPLE ARE GETTING STUPIDER EVERY DAY, RELATIVELY SPEAKING.
THE COMPLEXITY OF THE WORLD IS INCREASING GEOMETRICALLY.
S. Adams
BUT YOUR ABILITY TO LEARN IS AT THE SAME SLOW TRICKLE IT HAS ALWAYS BEEN.
INFORMATION IS GUSHING TOWARD YOUR BRAIN LIKE A FIREHOSE AIMED AT A TEACUP.
YOU'RE AT A CROSSROADS IN HISTORY. EVEN THE SMARTEST AMONG YOU HAS BECOME "FUNCTIONALLY STUPID."
8/18/96 © 1996 United Feature Syndicate, Inc.
YOUR ONLY HOPE IS TO CHOOSE A LEADER WHOSE VISION CAN PENETRATE THE THICK FOG OF HUMAN INCOMPETENCE.
DOGBERT FOR SUPREME RULER OF EARTH!!
DO YOU WANT MY OPINION?
WHAT ARE THE ODDS OF THAT?

I'VE HIT THE GLASS CEILING. I'LL NEVER BE PROMOTED AGAIN.

THAT'S BECAUSE YOU'RE NOT WILLING TO "PLAY THE GAME." YOU HAVE TO LOOK AND ACT LIKE THE PERSON WHO CAN PROMOTE YOU.
S.Adams

OOO-LA LA!
THIS HAD BETTER WORK.
8/19/96 © 1996 United Feature Syndicate, Inc.(NYC)

MY IDEA IS THAT EVERYONE SHOULD BE REQUIRED TO USE SMALL FONTS. THAT WAY WE'LL SAVE DISK SPACE.

AND I'VE NOTICED THAT MANY PEOPLE USE ENTIRE COLONS IN SITUATIONS WHERE A SEMICOLON WOULD DO JUST FINE.
S.Adams

YOU'RE RIGHT. THAT WAS FUN.
THE REAL FUN IS WHEN HE DESCRIBES HIS NEW IDEAS AT THE NEXT STAFF MEETING.
8/20/96 © 1996 United Feature Syndicate, Inc.(NYC)

I INVENTED A NEW DATA ENCRYPTION PROGRAM CALLED P.H.B. WHICH STANDS FOR POINTY-HAIRED BOSS.

IT CONVERTS E-MAIL INTO MANAGER BABBLE. NOBODY CAN INTERCEPT AND DECODE MY PRIVATE MESSAGES WITHOUT THE KEY.
WHO WOULD WANT TO READ YOUR MESSAGES?
S.Adams

SOMEBODY MIGHT WANT TO READ MY MESSAGES. IT COULD HAPPEN!
AND MAYBE YOU SHOULD CARRY PEPPER SPRAY IN CASE SUPERMODELS TRY TO KISS YOU.
8/21/96 © 1996 United Feature Syndicate, Inc.(NYC)

I AM ONLY A LOWLY INTERN, BUT I SEE AN OBVIOUS SOLUTION TO YOUR PROBLEM.
S.Adams

JUST CLICK HERE... CLEAR YOUR BUFFERS AND INITIALIZE THE LINK... NOW USE THIS CODE PATCH FOR THE MEMORY LEAK.

THIS IS FUNNY IF YOU CONSIDER THAT YOUR SALARY IS TWICE AS MUCH AS MINE.
I'M LAUGHING ON THE INSIDE.
8/22/96 © 1996 United Feature Syndicate, Inc.

ASOK THE INTERN
I CAME IN OVER THE WEEKEND AND LOOKED AT THE DESIGN YOU'VE BEEN WORKING WITH ALL YEAR.
S.Adams

IT TURNS OUT THAT YOU COULD HAVE BUILT THE UNIT AT HALF THE COST WITH JUST ONE MINOR CHANGE.

IS IT TRUE I CAN WIN AWARDS FOR THIS SORT OF THING?
FETCH THE INTERNAPULT.
8/23/96 © 1996 United Feature Syndicate, Inc.(NYC)

I'M GOING TO USE BAD GRAMMAR MORE OFTEN.
S.Adams

MY LEADERSHIP WILL CHANGE THE LANGUAGE THROUGH THE PRINCIPLE OF COMMON USAGE.
TIM

AND I WON'T STOP UNTIL THE ENTIRE LANGUAGE IS REDUCED TO GRUNTING AND POINTING! BUWAHA-HA HA!!
I REALLY GOT RIPPED OFF BY THAT DOG OBEDIENCE SCHOOL.
TIM
8/24/96 © 1996 United Feature Syndicate, Inc.(NYC)

OUR SENIOR VICE PRESIDENT WILL BE DROPPING IN TODAY.
REMEMBER TO INCREASE YOUR LIES ACCORDINGLY.
LIES
BOSS LEVEL
S. Adams
AND DECREASE THE DETAILS YOU PROVIDE.
DETAILS
BOSS LEVEL
IF I THINK YOU'RE BEING TOO INFORMATIVE, I'LL SIGNAL BY FIDGETING.
JUST SAY EVERYTHING IS FINE, BUT WE NEED MORE FUNDING.
HERE HE COMES.
8/25/96 © 1996 United Feature Syndicate, Inc.
SORRY I'M LATE. HOW IS EVERYONE?
I'M NOT SAYING.
I'M FINE, BUT I NEED MORE FUNDING.
I HAVE A WIDE VARIETY OF SUPER POWERS.
I FEEL A SUDDEN, URGENT NEED TO UNLOAD MY STOCK OPTIONS.
FIDGET FIDGET.

CATBERT THE HR DIRECTOR
MORALE IS LOW BECAUSE THE EMPLOYEES ARE UNDERPAID.

YOU CAN COMPENSATE BY HAVING MORE FREQUENT PERFORMANCE REVIEWS. THEY LOVE FEEDBACK.
S.Adams

THE HARDEST PART IS KEEPING A STRAIGHT FACE.
TELL ME AGAIN WHY I'D WANT MORALE TO BE HIGH?
8/26/96 © 1996 United Feature Syndicate, Inc.(NYC)

GOOD NEWS, ALICE. I'M GOING TO HAVE QUARTERLY PERFORMANCE REVIEWS TO BOOST MORALE.

WOW! IN ADDITION TO WORKING SIXTEEN HOURS A DAY IN THIS BIG BOX, NOW I'LL GET 300% MORE CRITICISM!
S.Adams

I'LL HAVE A CHANCE TO HEAR EMPLOYEE CONCERNS FOUR TIMES A YEAR.
I ASSUME COMPRE-HENSION WILL REMAIN ON THE BICEN-TENNIAL PLAN.
8/27/96 © 1996 United Feature Syndicate, Inc.(NYC)

AT FIRST I THOUGHT YOU COMMITTED ME TO AN IMPOSSIBLE DEADLINE. BUT I HAVE A THEORETICAL SOLUTION.

IT INVOLVES FLYING AROUND THE EARTH SO FAST THAT I TRAVEL BACK TO THE PAST.
S.Adams

AND THEN YOU'LL HAVE ENOUGH TIME?
NO, THEN I'LL GIVE YOUR PARENTS THIS PAMPHLET ON CONTRACEPTION.
8/28/96 © 1996 United Feature Syndicate, Inc.

... SO THE SALES-PERSON MADE AN IDIOTIC PROMISE TO OUR CUSTOMER. NOW IT'S MY JOB TO FIX IT.
THE BRAIN IS AN AMAZING THING.
S. Adams

ARE YOU SAYING THAT IF I USE THE UNTAPPED POWER OF MY BRAIN, THERE'S A SOLUTION?

NO, I'M SAYING MY AMAZING BRAIN FILTERED OUT YOUR BORING STORY SO I COULD ENJOY MY WALK.
8/29/96 © 1996 United Feature Syndicate, Inc. (NYC)

I'VE BECOME ONE OF THOSE PEOPLE WHO MISINTERPRETS EVERY-THING YOU SAY.
WHY?
S. Adams

WHY? ARE YOU SAYING THAT NOTHING SHOULD EVER CHANGE? MAYBE YOU SHOULDN'T BE SO RIGID.

THIS COULD BE VERY ANNOYING.
MAYBE YOU SHOULD SEE A THERAPIST FOR YOUR EMOTIONAL PROBLEM.
8/30/96 © 1996 United Feature Syndicate, Inc. (NYC)

I HEAR YOU'RE BECOMING AN ANNOYING PERSON WHO MISINTERPRETS EVERYTHING.
YES, I'M MORE ASSERTIVE.
S. Adams

I SAID ANNOYING, NOT ASSERTIVE.
APOLOGY ACCEPTED.

WHATEVER YOU DO, DON'T CLIMB IN THIS CLOTHES DRYER.
YEAH, IT DOES LOOK COZY IN THERE.
8/31/96 © 1996 United Feature Syndicate, Inc.